THE BACKGROUND OF
MODERN FRENCH POETRY

THE BACKGROUND OF
MODERN FRENCH POETRY

ESSAYS AND INTERVIEWS

BY

P. MANSELL JONES

Professor of Modern French Literature in the
University of Manchester

CAMBRIDGE
AT THE UNIVERSITY PRESS
1951
REPRINTED
1968

Published by the Syndics of the Cambridge University Press
Bentley House, 200 Euston Road, London, N.W. 1
American Branch: 32 East 57th Street, New York, N.Y. 10022

PUBLISHER'S NOTE

Cambridge University Press Library Editions are re-issues of out-of-print
standard works from the Cambridge catalogue. The texts are unrevised
and, apart from minor corrections, reproduce the latest published edition.

Standard Book Number: 521 07393 6
Library of Congress Catalogue Card Number: 52–7623

First published 1951
Reprinted 1968

First printed in Great Britain by The Carlyle Press, Birmingham, 6
Reprinted in Great Britain by John Dickens & Co. Ltd, Northampton

CONTENTS

PREFACE

THIS book brings together a series of related investigations pursued over a number of years into the major types of literary and prosodical influence involved in the progress of poetry in France from the time of Baudelaire. The first piece traces the migration of a powerful transcendental symbol from the sphere of pre-Romantic Illuminism into the deliberate appropriations and adaptations made by French writers and poets of a later period. The second attempts to estimate the limits and the value of what must be the most notorious literary influence in the poetry of the nineteenth century, the imposing but frequently miscalculated effects of Baudelaire's discovery of the work of Edgar Allan Poe. The third is more a study of innuendo than of authentic effect. Did Whitman 'influence' the Symbolists? It is far easier to say he did not than to explain why so many contemporaries of the movement suggested that he did. The first two chapters are concerned with operations ranging over ground covered at least in part of previous investigators. For the effects of *Leaves of Grass* I have had to rely on my own limited resources. The second part of the collection deals with the emergence of the *vers libre* from a hinterland of experiment and theory. While much of what is pertinent in French has been consulted in the attempt to elucidate this process, I have found nothing in English that throws light on the origins or on the nature of modern French free verse. Additional hints and notions on the foregoing topics were derived from contact with French poets of the post-Symbolist period, interrogated over thirty years ago.

All these pieces are presented as 'essays'. None claims to be an exhaustive treatment of a theme or an aspect. May this limitation

vii

diminish what traces they bear of those marks of hard labour which tend to remove the meticulous operations of much modern research from the interests of men of taste. I have attempted to keep a critical eye on such processes as have been appropriated here. It is often suggested that questions of source and influence have occupied the attentions of literary scholars too persistently during the past forty or fifty years. I agree that such studies have been disproportionately abundant in comparison with those that show a perception of values in the minds and works at each end of the line of influence. It is true, I fear, that discriminations of quality and judgment have been held too long in suspense out of excessive regard for scrupulous digressions into the 'backward and abysm' of literary history. But what occurs to one more frequently in ruminating over these matters is another sort of doubt: not that investigations of this kind go too far, but whether they go far enough? The role of influence as a determinant in literature and the arts cannot be denied. It is discussed or assumed universally nowadays, even by those critics who deplore the emphasis. Yet what is meant by 'influence' in these spheres? The word, in its most frequent use, is no master-key but a counter standing for a vague category into which is thrust with equal lack of discrimination samples of a complex phenomenon which has never been examined in its variations or in its essence. A large part of the problem presented by an influence in literature lies in the nature of literary influence itself. Similar doubts assail one about the methods habitually employed to detect or examine a specimen. The quest tends to operate in one direction only—away from the masterpiece. Yet the effort to retrogress toward the source remains largely gratuitous if the procedure is not inverted and pressed forward to appreciate the point at which source and influence are subsumed in the final synthesis. Considered in its full implication the problem of literary influence is an integral part of the problem of literary creation and this can never be differentiated—not to say solved—until what a writer of genius does with his material becomes the object of a more intuitive type of scholarship than is common today.[1]

I hardly hope that this collection will show much effect of these cautionary views. But I can assure the reader that, mainly through experimentation with the following examples, the conviction has grown that literary scholars for another half-century will not remain satisfied either with the methods or with the results of a type of research which, however conscientiously pursued, leaves too much of value out of account.

My thanks are due to the Editors of the *Modern Language Review* for allowing the use of two articles on the influence of Poe (*M.L.R.* July 1944 and October 1945) and of another on *The First Theory of the 'Vers Libre'* (April 1947). To the Editors of *French Studies* I am grateful for permission to include two pieces on Whitman's influence and the reminiscences of talks with French poets. (*F.S.* January, April and July 1948).

Help with proof-reading has been generously given by my colleagues, Mr J. H. Watkins, M.A., and Dr W. H. Barber. To Mr Watkins I am indebted for specific correction on details of importance. Through the courtesy of the Secretary of the Swedenborgian Society I was able to consult Rev Eric A. Sutton, M.A., B.D., Principal of New Church College, who has kindly permitted quotation from a letter, the interest of which may be found to extend beyond the limits of this work. Gratitude must finally be recorded for the constant attentions of officers of the Cambridge University Press.

P.M.J.

BANGOR

July 1951

[1] The type, I suggest, was finely realised in J. Livington Lowes' *The Road to Xanadu*. But no one interested in the problem should miss Mr T. S. Eliot's recent 'Talk on Dante' (*Adelphi*, First Quarter, 1951).

PART ONE

THREE MAJOR INFLUENCES

Correspondances

La Nature est un temple où de vivants piliers
Laissent parfois sortir de confuses paroles;
L'homme y passe à travers des forêts de symboles
Qui l'observent avec des regards familiers.

Comme de longs échos qui de loin se confondent
Dans une ténébreuse et profonde unité,
Vaste comme la nuit et comme la clarté,
Les parfums, les couleurs et les sons se répondent.

Il est des parfums frais comme des chairs d'enfants,
Doux comme les hautbois, verts comme les prairies,
—Et d'autres, corrompus, riches et triomphants.

Ayant l'expansion des choses infinies,
Comme l'ambre, le musc, le benjoin et l'encens,
Qui chantent les transports de l'esprit et des sens.

BAUDELAIRE

CHAPTER I

SWEDENBORG, BAUDELAIRE AND THEIR INTERMEDIARIES

I

'A COLOSSAL soul, he lies vast abroad on his times, uncomprehended by them, and requires a long focal distance to be seen.' Emerson's remark, uttered three-quarters of a century after Swedenborg's death, was prophetic. Within the century that has elapsed since he lectured at Manchester on *Swedenborg; or the Mystic*, many observers have attempted to get the northern seer into focus with a view to estimating the effect of his doctrine. Its influence was curiously at work even when Emerson spoke and in directions he could hardly have perceived. In the year his lecture was delivered (1847) a young French poet who was ultimately to show awareness of the essayist's ideas—and whose Icarus-like temperament and fate might conceivably have attracted the transcendental sage—had published a story called *La Fanfarlo*, in which Swedenborg's name occurs in a far less propitious context than it has in *The Fall of the House of Usher*, one of those tales of Poe which he subsequently translated. This interest was to grow and penetrate to the roots of his imagination, thrusting up a mystical blossom or two among the maladive flowers of his verse and enabling him to formulate a supernatural theory of poetic language.

How Baudelaire came to know anything of Swedenborg, how direct and precise his knowledge was and what use he ultimately made of it, are questions that have already been raised, but by no means completely answered. So voluminous is the work of the

Swedish naturalist turned mystic, so devious were the ways through which his influence ramified and so personal the reactions of each of his French admirers that, leaving unresolved problems of date and contact outside our purview, we may yet find much to reap in fields only partly harvested and something, perhaps, to say about the methods of reaping.

For a considered exposition of his doctrine Swedenborg recommended certain parts of his treatise on *Heaven and Hell*, published, as he tells us with characteristic precision, in London in the year 1758. It was Roderick Usher's choice and it seems likely that the work was known to Baudelaire. Among its main tenets are these:

> The Universal Heaven, and every part of it, resembles a Man, because it exists from the Divine Humanity of the Lord.
> There is a Correspondence of all things in Heaven with all things in Man.
> There is a Correspondence of Heaven with all things of Earth.

The radical anthropomorphism of Swedenborg's view, deduced from the inability of man or angel to conceive the Infinite, reappears in the asseveration that correspondence may be seen in the human face.[1] The doctrine is inclusive. Correspondence reaches not only downward to man and earth; the heavens themselves correspond to one another. And all things have their divine counterparts exact to the veriest detail. As Emerson complained, Swedenborg is 'superfluously explanatory'. Claiming that 'the universal heaven resembles one man, and that it is in the form of a man, and is therefore called the Grand Man', the seer proceeds to assert that 'the angelic societies, of which heaven consists, are consequently arranged like the members, organs and viscera in

[1] This notion was to be developed by J. G. Lavater in those elaborate but unscientific studies of physiognomy which interested the poets, among others, Blake and Baudelaire.

man; so that some are in the head, some in the breast, some in the arms and some in every particular part of these members'. Such specifications are multiplied with laborious precision.

The defects of Swedenborg's work from the literary point of view are obvious; but they should not mislead us. The stark rationality of its dogmatic conviction; the habit it displays of arguing logically from a basis of private revelation—much indeed is not even 'revealed' but deduced as effect from cause by a process of abstract reasoning; the suppression of mystery under the weight of concrete, commonplace or trivial detail—Hell consists of 'caverns' which are model 'workhouses'; there are two Londons beyond the grave, one for the good Londoners, one for the bad; from Heaven can fall 'a small piece of paper covered with Hebrew characters'; the rigours of its determinism, the over-definiteness of its formulas—what De Quincey called its 'matter-of-factness in execution'—all this provokes the question, how could a doctrine so dryly, categorically and meticulously presented have attracted the attention of the poets? Emerson himself put his finger on the contradiction: 'It is remarkable that this man, who, by his perception of symbols, saw the poetic construction of things, and the primary relation of mind to matter, remained entirely devoid of the whole apparatus of poetic expression, which that perception creates.' Or more curtly: 'In his profuse and accurate imagery is no pleasure, for there is no beauty.'

Yet there are positive implications in Emerson's remarks. Swedenborg had a prodigious faculty for myth-making and many of his inventions strike the mind's eye with force. The development of the theme, 'To grow old in heaven is to grow young', into a vision of women advancing with the millennia into an eternal, reversionary Spring; or the curious Fourth Memorial Relation, appended to a section of *The True Christian Religion*, in which the author, who has ready access to the heavenly state, tells how, approaching a group of spiritual beings who noticed that he faded out and reappeared (as a man might walking through light and shadow in a forest), he explained by means of 'three experimental proofs' the nature of the difference between what is spiritual and what is natural—these are but random examples of descriptive powers which range with complete assurance from the earthly to the heavenly plane and from one heaven to a higher.

The word 'correspondence' in its mystical connotation was not of course invented by Swedenborg. His use he defines as equivalent to the 'similitudes and comparisons' or 'parables' of Christ. A section like that on the Sacred Scriptures in *The True Christian Religion* is in a sense a treatise on the theory and practice of symbolic language, and the same notions are condensed in the chapters on Correspondence in *Heaven and Hell*. Incessant application of the doctrine makes the work of the Swedish mystic, with its repetitions and cross-references, and despite its 'immense and sandy diffuseness' budding here and there into oases of vision or mirage, an inexhaustible mine of analogies, in which poets, painters, preachers, mystagogues and demogogues have delved and plundered with more persistence and reward than has commonly been perceived.

Already when Baudelaire came first upon something by Swedenborg, a few generations of poets and painters had been at work on his exposition of Correspondences, transforming it from a mystical formula into a motif of great potency for literature and the arts.[1] In our own country Swedenborg's

---

[1] The reference throughout is strictly to Swedenborg's formulation. Correspondence in one form or another had haunted the mind of prophets and poets immemorially. See, for instance, E. M. W. Tillyard, *The Elizabethan World Picture*, pp. 77-93.

thought had attracted practical interest before the seer's death in 1772, and its appeal was to persist to the time of Carlyle, the Brownings and Coventry Patmore. 'His works,' said William Blake, who was brought up on them, 'are well worth the attention of painters and poets: they are the foundation for grand things.' In his book on Blake, Mr Basil de Selincourt has pointed to some of the ideas the poet owed to Swedenborg 'with much else that became most individual in his philosophy'; and he quotes:

> My eyes, more and more
> Like a sea without shore
> Continue expanding;
> Till the jewels of light,
> Heavenly men becoming bright
> Appear'd as One Man.[1]

Flaxman was an even more fervent admirer than Blake, who wavered in his allegiance. Coleridge earned the reputation of being a Swedenborgian, although his offer to write a life of the philosopher was rejected by the London Printing Society and the book he contemplated on the Doctrine of Correspondence was, like so many of his projects, never achieved. When in 1847 Emerson lectured in Manchester on 'Swedenborg; or the Mystic', he could speak of 'that slow but commanding influence which he has acquired'.[2]

Recent investigation has shown the recrudescence in France during the eighteen-thirties and 'forties of a religious interest in Swedenborg's teaching.[3] But this alone could hardly explain its

---

[1] Basil de Selincourt, *Blake*, p. 277.

[2] It may be of interest to note that in his fascinating study of the *Oxford Apostles*, Mr Geoffrey Faber contrasts the 'imagination' of Newman with the 'pictorial vision' of Swedenborg; the comparison turns to Swedenborg's advantage. See pp. 169, 170.

[3] See A. Viatte, 'Les Swedenborgiens en France de 1820 à 1830', *Revue de Littérature Comparée*, July-Sept. 1931.

B

attraction for Baudelaire. Other than direct agencies had been at work. As in England, the ferment there had already begun to operate on the precursors and founders of Romanticism.

Champfleury has left us a glimpse of the poet, with whom he was intimate, appearing with a book by Swedenborg under his arm and declaring with characteristic zest that nothing in all literature could stand comparison with it. The word '*correspondance*' recurs throughout Baudelaire's work, usually in italics, employed in a sense that leaves no doubt of its derivation. It is placed at the head of a sonnet which came to be regarded as a model for much in the Symbolist manner and which the later poets pondered deeply. Yet what differences separate the dogmatic exposition of the eighteenth-century mystic from the suggestive transformation of the idea in the 'celebrated' sonnet! Not only has a poet worked upon the theme, but he has treated it in the light of a number of other imaginative treatments, from which very probably he derived far more than from any direct contact with the original.

It may never be definitely known how Baudelaire came first upon the ideas of the Swedish mystic. Not that many of them could have been inaccessible in one form or another. From the end of the eighteenth century translations had appeared of some of Swedenborg's works and one or two more were turned into French during Baudelaire's lifetime. With his excellent Latin he could have dispensed with these. It seems clear, however, that he never imbibed strong doses of the doctrine, undiluted by commentators, and that what he took was very much according to prescription, combining ingredients from other Illuministic sources.

Fully to appreciate the background out of which Baudelaire's sonnet emerged, we must revert to certain developments in the eighteenth century which, like the beginnings of Romanticism, were alien in spirit to its dominant temper. Around the opposed peaks of rationalism and orthodoxy stretched an ocean of eccentric speculation; a chaos of conflicting superstitions one might be tempted to call it, had not some of its currents an obscure tradition, flowing through remote channels, clogged with obstructions and impurities, out of a mythical past. Both the radical notions and the modes of expression characteristic of the occult tradition and the literature it helped to produce, while being of widespread occurrence and incalculable antiquity, are usually traced to origins in Egypt and Chaldea. It was no doubt in part the exclusive intellectual emphasis of the century of Enlightenment which provoked these obscure latencies into flagrant or secretive reaction. Between 1600 and 1700 the growth of alchemistic literature had been enormous.[1] By the middle of the next century alchemy was being fused with freemasonry and throve alongside astrology, rosicrucianism, mesmerism, spiritualism and physiognomy on levels from which descent was rapid into charlatanry and hocus-pocus. Distinctions should be drawn in this connection between therapeutic or humanitarian aims and mercenary sleight of hand. Many of these fluid doctrines tended to coalesce on the spiritual side in dreams for the betterment of man and for his spiritual redemption. One group called themselves the Fusionists and attempted to compose an eclectic religion. But on the whole little cohesion and less consistency occurred between the nuclei of circumambient heresies, and sometimes they engaged in hostilities. It might be difficult to point to anything of permanent value that proceeded directly from these strange speculations and practices, in which hypothesis flourished unrestrained by experiment or criticism. But on the practical side there emerged a diversity of

[1] See Arturo Castiglioni, *Adventures of the Mind*, p. 254.

wonder-working cures, some of which were notoriously effective. Mesmer and Cagliostro flourished in the same century as Swedenborg and Pasqualis.

The Illuministic freemasonry of Martinez Pasqualis, who in 1754 founded the order of the Elus Cohens, was a ferment in the secret societies whose members played so prominent a part in the Revolution. Curiously enough there are signs that it also influenced the opposition. Through Williamoz of Lyons the ideas of Pasqualis affected the thought of Joseph de Maistre, whose traditionalism was based on a not uncommon amalgam of Catholic dogma and esoteric masonry. For Baudelaire Joseph de Maistre was 'le grand génie de notre temps—un voyant',[1] and the evidence is clear that *Les Soirées de St-Pétersbourg*, with its explicit reference to Illuminism, contributed important motifs to the making of *Les Fleurs du Mal*.[2] This is but one example. A generation or two of thinkers and writers like Lavater, whom Baudelaire called the 'angelic' man, Claude de Saint-Martin, Ballanche, Mme de Staël and Chateaubriand mediate between the Illuminists and the Romantics, and the filiation is prolonged in a line of Utopian reformers of the type of Saint-Simon, Fourier and Pierre Leroux.

The poets who drew from occult sources were not as a rule sectarians or adepts; their approach was tentative, partial or professional: they took what they wanted for their purposes as

[1] Letter to Alphonse Toussenel.

[2] Obvious examples are the poems, *Réversibilité* and *L'Héautontimorouménos*. M. René de Runéville is convinced that the poet's obsession with original sin is related to Pasqualis's insistence on the dogma, and finds in the opening phrase of the 'Correspondances' sonnet a reminiscence of the Temple in which Joseph de Maistre and other adepts of esoteric masonry used to meet and which was considered a replica and symbol of Nature. See *Les Cahiers d'Hermès* (Editions du Vieux Colombier, Paris, 1947), No. 1, p. 156.

writers. Most often contact was made through histories, abridgements, commentaries or mythological dictionaries. Of special interest to them, along with the attraction of certain doctrines and rituals, were the terminologies appropriated for the propagation of the revived creeds. All mysteries, esotericisms, arcana are alike in one thing, that reference can only be made to them in a language of symbols. The recrudescence of hermetical beliefs in the modern era presents no exception. Only of recent years have we begun to realize what resources of imaginative expression were offered by mythologies and fabulations such as those we have in mind to poets and artists for whom it was no longer congenial to exploit the classical stock or the Hebraic canon. Eighteenth-century Illuminism was one of the main sources from which Romantic poets and later on the Symbolists derived that profound sense of analogy which remains the key to their peculiar technique.

In his fascinating book on *Les Illuminés*, Gérard de Nerval makes this distinction: 'Vers 1770, les *martinistes*, les *swedenborgiens*, et enfin les illuminés, dont la doctrine fondée d'abord en Allemagne par Weishaupt, se répandait bientôt en France, où elle se fondait dans l'institution maçonique . . .' Here the application is too narrow: Spain had possessed Illuminati since the fifteenth century. The appellation was subsequently applied to various sects having, as M. René Guénon says, points of contact in the 'catholicity of the Tradition'.[1] It is not therefore surprising to find that certain poets accepted these diverse messages without appearing to feel a preference. It is possible, however, to separate out the particular repercussion of such messages upon the thought of those poets who found in them a prefiguration of modes of knowledge which their personal experience had led

[1] See *Les Cahiers d'Hermès*, No. 1, p. 171.

them to elaborate. The ideal example of an eclectic taste in esoteric matters was Gérard de Nerval. In *Aurélia*, it was recently claimed, he lives through all the myths of humanity by way of initiation. His experience is a mode of *askesis* through Illumination which at times reminds us of the spiritual pilgrimage of the precocious Rimbaud, and he had a similar sense of mission.[1] Of his learning in occult literature there can be little doubt. Reference to libraries of the kind are made more than once in *Les Illuminés*. The preface admits a direct debt to an assortment of curious volumes relegated to a loft after an uncle of the author's had become a deist. This may have been the set—'la tour de Babel en deux cents volumes'—which was placed at his disposal in Dr Blanche's clinic, where he received treatment before his death; and we shall see yet another mystical library playing its role in the case of Balzac. In one set probably, in the other admittedly, works by Swedenborg figured. His example was predominant. Yet it was but one of many influences of the sort reaching through the turmoil of the Revolution to affect the minds of French poets of the nineteenth century. We must be careful not to present Swedenborg's contribution as an isolated phenomenon —a ponderous meteor of Illuministic Latin impinging independently and unilaterally on the imagination of Baudelaire. The atmosphere in which the poet thought and wrote, if not that in which he lived, was instinct with notions of a supernatural character and he was familiar with several contemporary formulations.

Baudelaire, it has been dogmatically asserted, owed his acquaintance with Swedenborg's teaching to Gérard de Nerval. In a passage in *Aurélia*, which vies in beauty with the *Correspondances*

---

[1] 'Mon rôle me semblait être de rétablir l'harmonie universelle par art cabalistique, et de chercher une solution en évoquant les forces occultes de diverses religions' (*Aurélia*, II, vi).

sonnet itself, we find the phrase: 'Tout vit, tout agit, tout se correspond,' which unites the faith of Pythagoras with the favourite doctrine of the Northern sage. But precise estimates of priority are misleading and gratuitous in wide fields of general influence. Gérard de Nerval may, as we shall see, have shown Baudelaire how to adapt some of the ancient creeds to modern verse. But a far more striking, an unavoidable, example of the literary use of the Correspondence theme had forestalled the Illuministic work of Gérard de Nerval by ten to fifteen years.

II

Evidence seems to favour the view that it was Honoré de Balzac who provided, if not the first hint, at least the main stimulus to Baudelaire's interest in Swedenborg. For Baudelaire Balzac was essentially a 'poet', a 'passionate visionary'; and it was the realist turned visionary who served up the doctrine with a decidedly personal flavouring tinctured with extraneous ingredients to the point of contaminating the original. Unlike Poe, who scoffed at the Swedenborgians, though Baudelaire considered him an *illuminé*, Balzac was a declared believer, but *à sa façon* and, one may add, *à peu de frais*. There are reasons for believing that his direct knowledge of the Swedish mystic's extensive writings was limited to a volume of translated fragments known as the *Abrégé*, around which as a nucleus he fabricated a system of his own.[1]

Only of recent years has *Le Livre Mystique*, three of a series of

[1] Balzac, it seems, constructed his Swedenborgian edifice on the basis of one work only, an epitome of the doctrine of the New Jerusalem, composed of passages selected, translated and introduced by Daillant de la Touche, and published at Stockholm and at Strasbourg in 1788. See M. J. Van der Elst, 'Autour du Livre Mystique: Balzac et Swedenborg', *Revue de Littérature Comparée*, Jan.-Mar. 1930. It is probable that Baudelaire also knew

novels written mainly under the influence of Illuminist theories,[1] received much attention beyond the irritable side-glances of the critics. Brunetière, for instance, thought them hardly worth mentioning in his book on Balzac. Baudelaire (whose work Brunetière detested) must have read some if not all of these novels at an early date. It is known that Balzac figured among the writers that helped to enliven the voyage to the Indian Ocean imposed upon the young rebel by an irate step-father in 1841. The novelist's acquaintance with what W. B. Yeats called 'the modern visionary sects' is itself a story of some interest. That the author of the pseudo-Rabelaisian *Contes drôlatiques* should have turned to the composition of mystical romances is an odd but not inexplicable fact. Balzac's mother had possessed a library of modern mysticism. Her son's interest began there. It was to be stimulated from a remote quarter through an interchange of letters with a Russian admirer, Mme Eveline Hanska, the alluring 'Stranger', whom Honoré married the year before he died. *Séraphîta*, 'ce terrible Séraphîta', his supreme effort to adapt Swedenborg, was, he confessed, a struggle 'like that of Jacob's', sustained by a blend of mystical and sentimental aspiration. Dedicated to the lady, this literal labour of love failed to impress the recipient and the author's anxiety increased with the delay of acknowledgments.

Writing to Charles Nodier in 1832, Balzac advises him to find recruits for the *Revue de Paris*, 'parmi les platoniciens, les swedenborgistes, les illuminés, les martinistes, les bœhmenistes, les voyants, les extatiques, peuple-poète, essentiellement croyant,

this selection. In it the theme of Correspondence is illustrated by one passage only from *Heaven and Hell*, but a number of references are given in a footnote.

[1] The three novels comprising *Le Livre Mystique* of 1835 were *Louis Lambert*, *Séraphîta* and *Les Proscrits*.

acharné à comprendre et nullement à dédaigner!' He reminds Nodier that reprints have been made of several of those mystical works in which, as he says, the abyss of the infinite seems organized and where many intelligences either too weak or perhaps too strong love to lose themselves like wanderers in the subterranean passages of Rome. 'Realize', he adds, 'that I respect these works', and he gives a list—Swedenborg, Mme Guyon, Saint Theresa, Mlle Bourignon, Jacob Bohm (*sic*), etc.—of those to be found in bindings by his friend, Thouvenin, on a special shelf of his library. Five years later Balzac writes to Mme Hanska, confessing that, while politically a Catholic, he is not orthodox: ' . . . le swedenborgisme est ma religion avec l'augmentation que j'en fais de l'incompréhensible de Dieu . . .'.[1] Clear illustration of that blend of catholicism and Illuminism characteristic of several of the thinkers who attracted Baudelaire and to which a mind of his type was intimately addicted. Evidence too that Balzac means to amplify and transform his material. To Swedenborg, that is, to Balzac's notion of the master and his teaching, two of the novels are devoted, *Louis Lambert* (1832), parts of which are autobiographical, and *Séraphîta*, dated 1833-35. A glance at the content of these works will show something of the novelist's treatment of Illuministic material. But marks of the influence are also found in several others, notably in *Le Lys dans la Vallée*.[2]

Louis Lambert is the undramatic story of an eccentric boy whose spiritualistic interests bring him to the notice of Mme de Staël, by whom he is discovered reading *Heaven and Hell*. His celebrated benefactress provides an education at the Collège de

[1] These details are taken from F. Baldensperger, *Orientations Étrangères chez H. de Balzac* (Paris, 1922), ch. IX.

[2] See Régis Michaut, 'Baudelaire, Balzac et les Correspondances', *The Romanic Review*, Oct. 1938.

Vendôme, Balzac's old school, and the tale is mainly concerned with Lambert's maladjustment, his friendship with the author and his absorption in mystical speculation—'diction obscure, pleine d'abstractions et si active sur le cerveau, qu'il est certains livres de Jacob Boehm, de Swedenborg ou de madame Guyon dont la lecture pénétrante fait surgir des fantaisies aussi multi-formes que peuvent l'être les rêves produits par l'opium' (p. 29).[1] Multiform fantasies are characteristically what Balzac extracts from his contact with the mystics. Poor Lambert falls in love, becomes mad and is nursed by his mistress, whom the author persuades to transcribe her patient's stray thoughts. The tale ends with a selection. One of them (no. vii) deals with the funda-mental equivalence of sound, colour, perfume and form; it was recently compared by M. Henri Mondor to the second quatrain of the *Correspondances* sonnet. Others deal with unity, the dominant theme of the same quatrain. But we shall soon find closer parallels.

Compared with this sombre, unexciting story, *Séraphîta* is an astonishing *tour de force*. It claims to be 'une histoire vraiment céleste'. Of the seven chapters the first describing the movements of the strange couple, the hesitant, adoring Minna and the enig-matic, angelical Séraphîtus, as they pass along the ice-smooth ledges above the fiords is, read with unbiased eyes, an impressive *mise-en-scène*. Its delicate suggestions of mystery do not strain one's powers of acceptance as do the ambitious elevations of the last chapter and it is more consistently pictorial. This Norwegian 'Symphonie en blanc majeur' naturally won the admiration of Gautier. A precedent has been suggested in *Han d'Islande*. But I can find no ground for comparison except that the scenery in

---

[1] The references are to Calmann-Lévy's complete edition of Balzac's works, vol. XVII. Some revision of the texts had preceded this edition.

both novels is sub-arctic. Hugo's powers of description were at
their best unexcelled. But the treatment of landscape in his
Icelandic tale is vague and meagre compared with the precision
of Balzac's; that the topography is sometimes inexact does not
affect the brilliance of the glacial *décor*.

'Was it precisely because in Swedenborg alone the conscious
and the sub-conscious became one—as in that marriage of the
angels, which he has described as a contact of the whole being—
so completely one indeed that Coleridge thought Swedenborg
both man and woman?' W. B. Yeats's question, raised in *The
Trembling of the Veil*, suggests that the source of Balzac's experiment lay deeper than in the hermaphroditic nature of Fragoletta,
the central figure in Labiche's novel of that name, which, in a
letter to Mme Hanska, Balzac confessed he had in mind when he
created his asexual or, as he insisted, angelic personage. The
intimate ambiguity of Séraphîtus-Séraphîta's personality, though
not the principal theme of the romance, pervades what it has of
'plot' and affects the lovers in turn. Minna is lost in adoration of
the spiritual athlete, Séraphîtus, who guides her along the brink
of chasms. Wilfred, her sanguine *fiancé*, is distracted by the
female principle in Séraphîta, whom he hears expounding the
mystical doctrine before she passes from this life—a situation
which has been regarded as a sublimation of the robust author's
attitude to Eveline Hanska.

The third chapter gives Pastor Balzac, alias Becker, his chance
to expound. Setting out to tell the 'whole story of Swedenborg',
the pastor embarks on an extravaganza in which the fabulations
of the novelist invade and overweigh the original he claims to be
explicating.[1] The narrator insists less on the religious than on the

[1] The question of the novelist's fidelity to the philosopher was ably
discussed in an article published in the *Revue de Littérature Comparée*, to

poetical potential of the mystic's 'dazzling' work, which he characterizes as 'pleine de poésies en germe'. 'Pour les poètes et les écrivains', he adds in a significant phrase, 'son merveilleux est immense; pour les voyants, tout est d'une réalité pure . . . beaucoup de bons esprits n'admettent pas ses mondes où les couleurs font entendre de délicieux concerts, où les paroles flamboient, où le Verbe s'écrit en cornicules . . .'. The principle of synaesthesia is clearly perceived and differentiated. A like emphasis will be found in Baudelaire, but not, I think, in Swedenborg. The 'cornicules' or little curved lines used by the angels in their handwriting are indeed described in *The True Christian Religion* (§278) and are referred to again in *Heaven and Hell* (§260). But the reader reverting to the appropriate paragraphs will find no mention of worlds where colours produce concerts or where speech catches fire. And I doubt whether exact counterparts to Balzac's words could be found elsewhere in Swedenborg's writings.

These points are amplified in the fourth chapter, a Balzacian variation on quasi-Swedenborgian themes, placed as a testament or apologia on the lips of the central personage before his/her assumption. It is a doctrine of Correspondence; but it is rooted in a special sense of the unity, the *homogeneity*, of things, which the novelist derived, not I think directly from the Swedish mystic, but from the Swiss pastor, Lavater, to whom apparently Baudelaire will be indebted for it in turn.[1]

Séraphîta's exposition revolves ingeniously round a faith in

which we have already referred (p. 11, n.1). The author, M. J. Van der Elst, gave examples of judgments passed on *Séraphîta* by members of the Swedenborgian New Church of America. 'It glitters but is not gold' was one verdict; another condemned the novel as 'only a caricature' of the faith.

[1] See Professor G. T. Clapton, 'Lavater, Gall et Baudelaire', *Revue de Littérature Comparée*, Apr.-June, July-Sept. 1933.

the essence of things which has been shattered or effaced by Science. Her attitude involves an attack on scientific progress as dualistic and a definition of the doctrine of Correspondence as fundamentally a doctrine of Unity. The key word recurs in different contexts.

'Donc, votre invisible univers moral et votre visible univers physique constituent une seule et même matière' (p. 184); 'tout est UN comme Dieu, et vous n'apercevez ni point de départ ni point d'arrivée' (p. 188); 'Pour savoir le sens vrai des lois phénoménales, ne faudrait-il pas connaître les corrélations qui existent entre les phénomènes et la loi d'ensemble' (p.199).

And the idea reappears in a characteristic form at the end of the discourse:

'En nommant Dieu le Créateur, vous le rapetissez; il n'a créé, comme vous le pensez, ni les plantes, ni les animaux, ni les astres; pouvait-il procéder par plusieurs moyens? n'a-t-il pas agi par l'unité de composition?' (p. 202).[1]

What finally seals the conviction of Wilfred and Minna is the realization of spiritual unity through the equivalence of sense impressions.

Ils comprirent les invisibles liens par lesquels les mondes matériels se rattachaient aux mondes spirituels. En se rappelant les sublimes efforts des plus beaux génies humains, ils trouvèrent le principe des mélodies en entendant les chants du ciel qui donnaient les sensations des couleurs, des parfums, de la pensée, et qui rappelaient les innombrables détails de toutes les créations, comme un chant de la terre ranime d'infimes souvenirs d'amour (p. 231).

It would be over-definite to affirm that these fragments of

[1] The remarkable development given to this idea includes a reference which differs from the one Baudelaire was to repeat: ' Comme l'a dit Swedenborg, *la terre est un homme!*' (*sic*).

Balzac's story offer a prior draft of the main precepts and examples condensed in Baudelaire's sonnet. But it is obvious that such passages present a combination of elements that would appeal strongly to the poet. The fundamental sense of analogy with the implied reference to Swedenborgian terminology; the conviction of unity in which the universal analogies have their beginning and their end; the expression or illustration of these basic principles in terms of the interfusion of sense impressions—one is tempted to say that all this crystallizes out in the lines:

> Comme de longs échos qui de loin se confondent
> En une ténébreuse et profonde unité,
> Vaste comme la nuit et comme la clarté,
> Les parfums, les couleurs et les sons se répondent.

But to any suggestion of exclusive indebtedness, whether to Balzac or Swedenborg through Balzac, obvious reservations must be made. For many years school manuals have stressed the poet's debt to Hoffmann for the dominant examples of synaesthesia with which the sonnet ends and have related them, as well as the purport of the four lines quoted above, to a phrase he took for his *Salon* of 1846 from the German writer's *Kreisleriana*, published nearly twenty years before *Séraphîta*. Reverting to the last quotation we made from the end of the novel, the scene of the Assumption, this too, it has been found, comes not from anything by Swedenborg but from a work by his French disciple, Claude de Saint-Martin's *Ministère de l'homme esprit*. Upon this *mélange* Balzac imposed his own form of language and it is the novelist's *formulation*, I suggest, that attracted the poet. As we shall see, the only part of the language of the sonnet which can definitely be called 'Swedenborgian' is the title and this, it has been suggested, may have been added some time after the poem was written. To certain aspects of Swedenborg's thought Baudelaire must, as I hope to show, have been intimately sensitive. But direct influence is far less visible in the sonnet than in certain other parts of his work.

The fourth poem of *Les Fleurs du Mal* is a curious and fascinating amalgam capable, like all symbols, of adapting itself to more than one mode of interpretation. It cannot be explained as a result of linear development. Drawing from multifarious elements in the soil and atmosphere of its background, it defies dogmatic analysis and confronts investigation with alternative 'proofs' which make the assertions of the unwary appear arbitrary or irrelevant. Yet diverse and ramifying as its roots appear to be, the poem is none the less a synthesis, a significant unit. Any implication of dispersion must be set against our method of analysis which carries inquiry back along the widening lines of those long echoes that converge and blend in the centre of the sonnet. Our conception of the sonnet as a whole, in relation to its background, has yet to be discussed. So far our inquiry has focused upon the sources of the second quatrain. The 'mystery' lies in the opening lines.

III

Vague insinuations of literary influence can have wondrous fortunes. Even in these days of precise method, they may flourish unratified and unchallenged—cherished by competent editors. The suggestion that a couplet from Poe's juvenile poem, *Al Aaraaf*, had some kind of effect on the production or the inception of Baudelaire's sonnet, *Correspondances*, appears to have been derived from one of the earliest of academic theses published on the relationship, in which the lines

> All Nature speaks and even ideal things
> Flap shadowy sounds from visionary wings. . .

were simply juxtaposed to the opening lines of the sonnet as examples of 'symbols' which the two poets see 'everywhere'.[1] The devoted Baudelairian editor M. Jacques Crépet accepted the comparison tentatively, under the persuasion, perhaps, of intermediary investigators who repeated it.[2] But in another edition of Baudelaire's complete works by Féli Gautier, continued by M. Y. G. Le Dantec, Crépet's phrase was taken over as a statement made with an air of authority it could never have been intended to wear. In all probability the whole series of assumptions misses the obvious. Baudelaire's acquisitive powers were considerable; but they were not obliged to reach across the Atlantic for material which lay at hand. His models for much of the mysterious language of the sonnet were autochthonous and germane to the French Romantic tradition. In one of his *Premières Méditations* Lamartine had written:

> Dieu caché, disais-tu, la nature est ton temple!

A chapter in M. Jean Pommier's book, *La Mystique de Baudelaire*, tabulates the significant parallels to the symbolic language with which the sonnet in question begins. The examples I shall quote do not exhaust those given by him or by other French commentators. In the notes to the best contemporary edition of *Les Fleurs du Mal* (Librairie José Corti, 1942)[3] the lineage of the phrase, 'La Nature est un temple', is traced back to Diderot, Gassendi and through Montaigne to Plutarch. Even these ramifying detections miss the presence of the phrase 'le temple de la nature' in Robespierre's speeches and of a similar locution in Ruskin's

[1] Arthur S. Patterson, *L'Influence d'Edgar Poe sur Charles Baudelaire*, Grenoble, 1903.

[2] The reference here is to the *Œuvres Complètes* (Edition Conard, 1922-39), *Les Fleurs du Mal*, p. 412.

[3] Edition critique établie par Jacques Crépet et Georges Blin. Here Patterson's 'find' is ascribed to a later investigator.

Modern Painters (1844). Recurring increasingly between these limits, it may safely be regarded as one of the perennial romantic clichés produced by the diffusion of religious sentiment over the natural scene.

In 1845 Abbé Constant, an Illuminist later known as Éliphas Lévi, had in a collection called *Les Trois Harmonies* celebrated universal analogy under a title to be used by Baudelaire with omission of the article. Constant's poem, *Les Correspondances*, contains stanzas of this type:

> Formé de visibles paroles
> Ce monde est le songe de Dieu;
> Son verbe en choisit les symboles,
> L'esprit les remplit de son feu...

But M. Pommier attaches more importance to that sonnet by Gérard de Nerval, 'Homme, libre penseur...', which figures in the *Oxford Book of French Verse*. Its capricious author changed the title of his 'vers dorés' more than once; but the poem remains a variation on its Pythagorean epigraph, 'Eh quoi! tout est sensible'. A notable line from the sestet, warning us of the disquieting vigilance with which inanimate things are endowed—

> Crains dans le mur aveugle un regard qui t'épie

may have induced the later poet to charge the auditive imagery of his opening lines with a similar implication of animistic watchfulness:

> La Nature est un temple où de vivants piliers
> Laissent parfois sortir de confuses paroles;
> L'homme y passe à travers des forêts de symboles
> *Qui l'observent avec des regards familiers.*

It is also possible, as M. Pommier observes, that certain lines and images of a visionary quality in Hugo's earlier poems may have given hints to both later poets. But the interfusion of natural and religious impulses is fundamental to Romanticism, and the correlation of the corresponding symbols had been notably exemplified in the year Hugo was born. Chateaubriand's comparison of the Gothic Cathedral to a grove of forest trees, perhaps the most familiar fragment in his *Génie du Christianisme*, invites more attention in this connection than the passing reference it receives from M. Pommier.

It seems odd, indeed, that half a century's effort to dissolve the originality of Baudelaire into a multiplicity of debts to lesser men should have shown relatively little curiosity about his relationship to one of the founders of the Romantic tradition. *Le Génie du Christianisme*, that source-book for so much in modern French literature, remains, despite its presentation of an outmoded Christian aestheticism, surprisingly readable through the skill with which it is written, provided we do not expect what it was not intended to offer—theological argument or dogmatic proof. The great Catholic pre-Romantic with his recovered sense of mystery in nature and in destiny, deepened by the conviction of original sin and redemption; his instinctive acceptance of dogma accompanied by a relative indifference to personal ethics; above all, his insistence on an ideal beauty—how could the assimilative perceptions of the author of *Les Fleurs du Mal* fail to recognize a special precursor in so imposing a master, to whom, in the sequel, many poets of the Baudelairian tradition appear to have been indebted for ideas as well as for imagery?

Turn for instance to the second chapter, *De la Nature du Mystère*. The germs of Symbolist theory emerge in a phrase like this: 'Le secret est d'une nature si divine, que les premiers hommes de l'Asie ne parlait que par symboles. A quelle science revient-on sans cesse? à celle qui laisse toujours deviner et qui fixe nos regards sur une perspective infinie.' Such a passage contains a hint that can be seen developing through Sainte-Beuve into the only popular pronouncement Mallarmé ever made when, defining his method to the journalist, Jules Huret, he contrasted it in simple terms with that of the Parnassians: '*Nommer* un objet, c'est supprimer les trois quarts de la jouissance du poème qui est faite du bonheur de deviner peu à peu; le *suggérer*, voilà le rêve. C'est le parfait usage de ce mystère qui constitue le symbole . . .'. But read in conjunction with other phrases in the same chapter— 'Les sentiments les plus merveilleux sont ceux qui nous agitent un peu confusément'; or 'nous allons chercher ces forêts, berceaux de la religion, ces forêts dont l'ombre, les bruits et le silence sont remplis de prodiges'—and it is not Mallarmé who comes first to mind but his predecessor, Baudelaire. When in the sequel Chateaubriand reaches his main subject, *Beaux-Arts et Littéra-ture*, he reverts to the theme of the forest-cradle of religion and expands it into the famous chapter in which, I suggest, the poet of *Correspondances* may have found much to think over, much perhaps, as Du Bellay would say, to make his own.

The chapter on the Gothic Churches[1] is, like the rest of the work, expository in design, part of an original plan to demon-strate the aesthetic potential of the Hebrew and Christian mysteries. Here the exposition is based on a comparison between the nave and the grove which is used with the balanced freedom of a simile. The sonnet on the other hand shows, at least in its opening lines, a high degree of metaphorical density. Baude-laire, one of a vast progeny, appears to have responded, if not as fully, perhaps as profoundly as any of Chateaubriand's disciples

---

[1] *Le Génie du Christianisme*, Troisième Partie, Livre Premier, ch. VIII. The attraction this passage had for Baudelaire is further illustrated in a later sonnet, *Obsession* (1860). See *Les Fleurs du Mal* (Edition Corti), p. 425.

to the spirit as well as to the letter of the doctrine. For the case to be examined is not just a matter of borrowing detached words or phrases or even of appropriating a sequence. It is one that shows the same kind of language used, if only for a limited space, in a similar spiritual content.

Actually these few paragraphs of Chateaubriand's description provide an almost exhaustive glossary of the terms used in the first three lines of the sonnet. The reader who may wish to test this assertion should run his eye along the phrases that begin with the words: 'L'ordre gothique . . .', not omitting the note appended by the author which ends with the phrase: 'mais nous aimons mieux encore rapporter son origine [i.e. of the cathedral] à la nature'. He will recognize all but one of the significant words used by Baudelaire occurring in the following order: *nature* (footnote) . . . *forêts* . . . *temples* . . . *piliers* . . . *confuses* (*rumeurs*), along with developments and modulations in which they recur, the series of paragraphs beginning (as the sonnet does) with the plastic images, instinct with a mysterious yet natural vitality, and acquiring audible effects as they proceed: 'L'architecture chrétienne, non contente de bâtir des forêts, a voulu, pour ainsi dire, en imiter les murmures'. Nor could it be maintained that Baudelaire's ephithet 'vivant', and the word 'symbole', have no kind of equivalent in the suggestive language of his predecessor. A phrase like 'bâtir des forêts' is metaphorical and the whole passage is concerned with an animated and vocal architecture.

Yet even if it be conceded that the possibilities of a serious debt are here disclosed, we must not fall into the frequent error of considering a relationship like this as exclusive. Other precedents have been revealed from which the poet could as easily have drawn. He might be indebted to one or to many; he might

24

be unconsciously indebted to all, even had he convinced himself of his debt to one alone. The insuperable difficulty of the search for sources, where no evidence is sufficiently definite or 'clinching' enough to rout competition, becomes apparent and one is tempted to question the utility of pressing such inquiries beyond clearly ascertainable limits.

> Who that shall point, as with a wand, and say,
> 'This portion of the river of my mind
> Comes from yon fountain. . .'

Wordsworth's question is a corrective. It is possible of course for a definable debt to be incurred, if not always to an 'original', at least to an intermediary, that is, as I have suggested, to a prior formulation. Such a stage may be as far as the 'proof' of an influence can usefully be carried. Yet to go no further than that, it might be argued, is to trace the effect to a *form*, not to a content. To which I should reply with the question: What literary purpose is served by attempting to track down a content capable of such prolonged transmigrations, such innumerable metamorphoses as the notion we are dealing with? For this at least is clear: our investigation, even within its restricted limits, points to something like a tradition, an immemorial mystical tradition, unorthodox because boundless, passing through incessant modifications and to which Baudelaire appears to be indebted, so to speak, indiscriminately and in ways too subtle, too obscure, too subterranean to be capable of differentiation or of precise demonstration. This tradition, in its later modes—remembering the type of content we have to deal with and the type of poet—I venture to call the Illuminist-Romantic tradition; and it would not be difficult to find further evidence of it in quarters which might seem remote enough from those we have been considering here.[1]

[1] An interesting comparison might for instance be established between

But now for a final question, if there can be any finality about a subject of this kind. Practically every word of importance in the sonnet has been accounted for in terms of the language used in similar contexts by immediate predecessors. Do the claims investigators have made on behalf of Chateaubriand, Hoffmann, Balzac, Hugo, Gérard de Nerval and Poe, and we may as well add Lavater and Saint-Martin, obliterate Swedenborg, leaving to his account an isolated title? Not necessarily. Something of the mystic's thought, if not of his phraseology, may have circulated through the mind of every member of the series. Nor will it be possible to deny on further evidence that an influence so penetrating and expansive co-operated at a more or less unconscious level with Baudelaire's impulses. The poet, as I have said, is predominantly interested in the *verbal* application of the theory of Correspondences. A section like that on the Sacred Scriptures in *The True Christian Religion* would have special attraction for him. There is no evidence that he knew it; but he could have found something of the same kind in *Heaven and Hell*.[1] Like the rest of Swedenborg's work, the section I refer to is arranged in paragraphs under definite rubrics. One of them (§220) reads: '*Truths and goods in their ultimates, such as are in the literal sense of the Word, were represented by the curtains, vails and pillars of the tabernacle*'. Here Swedenborg is commenting on Exodus, XXVI, 1, 31 and 36.[2] From the fact that 'the tabernacle which Moses built in the wilderness represented heaven and the church', he

the examples we have been studying and Wordsworth's lines on the *Simplon Pass* (composed 1799 [? 1844], published 1845). What would not an ardent quester of parallels be able to make of a comparison with Nerval's sonnet, if only the 'rocks that muttered' and the 'crags that spake' had also been endowed with eyes to see!

[1] See especially pp. 234-64 passim.

[2] The next paragraph refers to the temple at Jerusalem (I Kings, v, 7, 29, 30).

characteristically assumes that 'all the things contained in the tabernacle . . . represented and signified the holy things of heaven and of the church'. Hence, he concludes, 'the ultimates of the tabernacle as the curtains, the vails, *the pillars . . . signified the ultimates of the Word*'.

Have we not here, one might be tempted to ask, in the words I have italicized, the rock-foundation of Baudelaire's oracular pillars? Support for such a suggestion might be found by looking a little further into the context. Not only are the pillars in each case symbols of speech, but it is also worth noting that Swedenborg's paragraph ends, just as Baudelaire's sonnet ends, with a series of sense impressions which are 'correspondences': 'fine linen signified truth from a spiritual origin; blue (*hyacinthinum*), truth from a celestial origin; purple, celestial good; double-dyed scarlet, spiritual good . . .'.

It is clear that symbols of the same kind occur in the same order in the paragraph and in the sonnet. Yet this does not in itself permit one to speak of a specific debt. One has no reason to doubt that the poet knew something at first hand of Swedenborg. But neither external nor internal evidence seems strong enough to enable one to affirm that he had the above or any other paragraph of Swedenborg's work in mind when he wrote the sonnet. The differences will, of course, be felt to be considerable. The mystic is precise; the poet imprecise. The one expounds; the other suggests. Swedenborg is intent on what is signified; Baudelaire on the phenomenon of signification: the 'celebrated' sonnet is one of the chief prototypes of the introverted, esoteric symbolism to be elaborated by Mallarmé. There is an even more specific contrast to note. Swedenborg's language is biblical and familiar. Baudelaire's could have been familiar only to readers of some of his predecessors: Chateaubriand, Balzac, Nerval,

Hoffmann or Swedenborg himself. The language of the sonnet has already taken almost a century to explicate.

Yet the resemblance I have drawn attention to may be more than a coincidence. The interest I derive from this exercise is not that of tracking a specimen of literature linearly back to its 'source'. It lies in the general implication that minds of a mystical type resemble one another in their modes of reaction and expression, and never more than when brought into contact with an ancient corpus of archetypal symbols. They will tend in reproducing such symbols to arrange them in similar ways, though not without interesting divergences. Such divergences are important, especially in the case of poets and artists whose claims to 'originality' may be related to them. And, as I have already suggested, in fields of influence whose scope and antecedents are numerous and remote, it may often be unprofitable to go in search of the *fons et origo* before we have examined the more immediate impact of one writer's phraseology upon another's. Fundamentally of course the problem of influence is far more than a matter of verbal resemblance or parallelism. But the quest of such an influence as that of a mind like Swedenborg's, whether he be called a mystic or a mystagogue, on a poet, I should like to insist, on a poet of mystical tendency like Baudelaire, is one that leads backwards almost indefinitely to forms that have been for ages mobile realizations of the symbolized knowledge or experience of the human spirit as it gropes through a mysterious universe. Swedenborg, as we saw, professed to be expounding Exodus. The idea of the vocal or oracular pillar occurs in a special form in one of the most august passages in Old Testament literature, that about the appearance of the Lord to Moses at the door of the tabernacle: 'And it came to pass, as Moses entered into the tabernacle, the cloudy pillar descended, and stood at the door of the tabernacle, and the Lord talked with Moses'. (Exodus, xxxiii, 9). It is unlikely that any sensitive modern European, whether a Bible-reader or not, could have completely escaped the vibrations set up by such a phrase as that. In the case of men like Chateaubriand and Baudelaire we may assume that the scriptural sources had been, to say the least, unconsciously assimilated. What, we might ask, are the temples raised by these men of mystical imagination but reconstructions made long after the limits fixed by Christ's prophetic computation of three days? For the most powerful temples of all are built of words, and the moderns have often taken words from the ancients and used them for their own constructions. Baudelaire is not thinking of Exodus or of Christ or of Swedenborg when he writes:

La Nature est un temple où de vivants piliers;

he is writing his own kind of poem. And it will be possible, I think, to show that he will not be thinking specifically of Swedenborg even when he adapts his language with far more deliberation than by giving a sonnet the title *Correspondances*. An examination of other contexts in which the mystical term appears persuades us that what the poet-critic is ultimately concerned with is less the mystery of universal counterparts than that, equally sublime, of the creative artist's task. This he conceives as the inspired manipulation of symbolical language; and in this sense the poem is indeed, as M. Pommier claims in words borrowed from Baudelaire, a 'catéchisme de haute esthétique'.

IV

If we look into the poet's various uses of the word *correspondance*, we shall find that none of the contexts in which it occurs is concerned with a restatement of Swedenborg's doctrine, to which

Baudelaire refers once only and *en passant*. As usual when he appropriates, he concentrates on the application. The only place where he makes a general statement, not of the doctrine, but of the essential phenomenon of analogy or symbolism is the sonnet itself to which he attaches the mystical title, but which, as we have seen, is compact of imagery drawn more or less unconsciously from literary precedents—to the whole of which he gives a turn in accordance with his dominant supernatural aesthetic. The Swedish mystic had no such interest and the difference between their intentions will be clear. Swedenborg propounds a mystical theory of universal relationships; Baudelaire concentrates on a supernatural conception of artistic perception based on analogy. Turn for a moment to his article on Wagner (1860). After a paragraph definitely devoted to the problem of synaesthesia regarded from the standpoint of music, he employs the first two quatrains, the most general lines of his own sonnet, to illustrate the point. This suggests that he intends the sonnet as a meditation on the mysteries of universal analogy with special reference to the experience of the artist—the true artist, the reader and interpreter of the symbolic script of creation. As early as 1856 Baudelaire had inserted his views, evidently not recent convictions, in the letter to Toussenel, which bears comparison with Rimbaud's *Lettre du Voyant*:

Il y a bien longtemps que je dis que le poète est *souverainement* intelligent, qu'il est *l'intelligence* par excellence—et que *l'imagination* est la plus *scientifique* des facultés, parce que seule elle comprend *l'analogie universelle*, ou ce qu'une religion mystique appelle *la correspondance*.[1]

In the best book available on the thought of Baudelaire,

[1] Charles Baudelaire, *Correspondance Générale* (Editions Conard, 1947), vol. I, p. 367.

M. Georges Blin points with abundant examples to the 'degree of banality' reached by the principle of Correspondence by the time the French poet took it up: 'Tous ceux dont Baudelaire s'inspire, tous ceux qu'il a pratiqués ou connus, tous posent ou exposent cette théorie des correspondances'.[1] M. Blin makes a subtle distinction between correspondence and synaesthesia, opposing one notion to the other. Much simplified, his contention is that the former operates 'vertically' between things on earth and their heavenly counterparts; whereas synaesthesia works horizontally between sense impressions on the earthly plane. The Symbolist school, he claims, identified symbolism with synaesthesia; whereas true poetic symbolism is a mode of correspondence.

These distinctions are instructive, and it would be difficult to question their general applicability to Baudelaire. But the more closely one examines the poet's uses of the words *correspondance* and *correspondant* in their contexts, the more it seems clear that Baudelaire is interested practically, that is, as a poet and critic, not so much in the 'vertical' theory as in the 'horizontal' phenomena. Baudelaire does not confine himself to the interfusion of sense impressions; but his larger treatments of artistic perception are dominated, as I think we shall see, by modes of analogy or symbolism which work on planes of their own. The interrelation of planes may be implied; it is never emphasized. The poet, once again, is interested in aesthetic rather than in Swedenborgian equivalents.

A few more instances of his use of the key word may bring this out. One of the earliest examples will be found in his article on the *Exposition Universelle de 1855*, where he speaks of the 'immense clavier des correspondances'. The phrase is used in

[1] Georges Blin, *Baudelaire* (N.R.F.), p. 107. Note the references given to the phrase quoted above.

connection with his sense of the diversity of beauty. The adaptable critic has the 'divine grace of cosmopolitanism'; the narrow pedantic judge is likened to a pianist whose fingers cannot move lightly over 'l'immense clavier'. At the risk of forcing a point, I note that a keyboard is horizontal.

Perhaps the most charming of all variations on the mystical theme will be found in the *Poèmes en prose* (XVIII) under the title of *Invitation au Voyage*, a version of one of the best known of the *Fleurs du Mal*. The key to the following phrase, addressed to the beloved—'Fleur incomparable, tulipe retrouvée, allégorique dahlia, c'est là, n'est ce pas, dans ce beau pays si calme et si rêveur, qu'il faudrait aller vivre et fleurir? Ne serais-tu pas encadrée dans ton analogie, et ne pourrais-tu pas te mirer, pour parler comme les mystiques, dans ta propre *correspondance*?'— occurs a little later: 'Ces trésors, ces meubles, ce luxe, cet ordre, ces parfums, ces fleurs merveilleuses, c'est toi . . .'

No hint here of a plane above the level of earth and sea. Commentators have identified the journey's end with Holland, that most horizontal of countries.[1] We can conclude, I think, that Baudelaire's imagination, though that of an idealist, moves far more easily on the horizontal plane of analogies, provided we assume with him that all analogies are involved in a universe which is *one* to the poet's perception—'les choses', as he says in the article on Wagner, 's'étant toujours exprimées par une analogie réciproque, depuis le jour où Dieu a proféré le monde comme une complexe et indivisible totalité'.

The word *correspondance* occurs twice in the study of Edgar Allan Poe prefixed to the second collection of tales, translated as the *Nouvelles Histoires Extraordinaires* (1857). Here the

[1] The choice of Holland as the ideal lover's resort may have been suggested by a curious phrase of Swedenborg's. See Pommier, *op. cit.* p. 30.

implication is definitely supernatural: 'C'est cet admirable, cet immortel instinct du Beau qui nous fait considérer la terre et ses spectacles comme un aperçu, comme une correspondance du Ciel'. The phrase is an interesting fusion of the American's aesthetic principle with pure Swedenborgian doctrine. The other phrase from the same piece defines Imagination as a quasi-divine faculty whose power it is to perceive immediately, and without relying on philosophic means, 'les rapports intimes et secrets des choses, les correspondances et les analogies'. This seems to revert to the plane of interrelated things. But in both cases it should be noticed the word is used, not of universal relationships as such, but specifically with reference to the powers of a poet. In these two instances the word (in the Conard edition) lacks the customary italics, but recovers them when one of the passages is repeated verbatim in an article on Théophile Gautier. Here again the idea of Correspondence is applied to the essentials of a poet's operations. But now it is used to develop a mystical conception of poetic language, metaphor, the *verbum*. In fact a complete theory of Symbolism is epitomized in dealing with the forerunner of the Parnasse!

Si l'on réfléchit qu'à cette merveilleuse faculté Gautier unit une immense intelligence innée de la *correspondance* et du symbolisme universels, ce répertoire de toute métaphore, on comprendra qu'il puisse, sans cesse, sans fatigue comme sans faute, définir l'attitude mystérieuse que les objets de la création tiennent devant le regard de l'homme. Il y a dans le mot, dans le *verbe*, quelque chose de *sacré* qui nous défend d'en faire un jeu de hasard. Manier savamment une langue, c'est pratiquer une espèce de sorcellerie évocatoire.

This passage should be compared with a more elaborate one from the article on Victor Hugo, usually considered Baudelaire's finest piece of critical writing. Here the poet's conception of analogy and its uses in poetry receives fullest development. After referring to some examples of analogical formulae—Fourier's, Lavater's, Swedenborg's—which establish the symbolic nature of the universe, he claims that the poet is the being who understands such formulae; he is the translator or decipherer of nature's hieroglyphics. The phrase used of Swedenborg in contrasting him with Fourier is worth noting:

> D'ailleurs Swedenborg, qui possédait une âme plus grande, nous avait déjà enseigné que *le ciel est un très-grand homme*; que tout, forme, mouvement, nombre, couleur, parfum, dans le *spirituel* comme dans le *naturel*, est significatif, réciproque, converse, *correspondant*.

This brief epitome is the only account of the doctrine to be found in the French poet's works.[1] But note how Baudelarian is the series, *forme, mouvement, nombre, couleur, parfum*! Swedenborg shows no concern with abstractions or qualities of this kind; he is absorbed in concrete replica. As the paragraph proceeds it is given the specific turn we have now come to expect:

> Si nous étendons la démonstration (non-seulement nous en avons le droit, mais il nous serait infiniment difficile de faire autrement), nous arrivons à cette vérité que tout est hiéroglyphique, et nous savons que les symboles ne sont obscurs que d'une manière relative, c'est-à-dire, selon la pureté, la bonne volonté ou la clairvoyance native des âmes. Or qu'est-ce qu'un poète (je prends le mot dans son acception la plus large), si ce n'est un traducteur, un déchiffreur?

The argument, distinctive as it is, terminates with a touch of meticulous absolutism which recalls the manner of the Swedish doctrinaire:

[1] Even here Baudelaire may be recalling Swedenborg through the intermediary of Balzac. See Pommier, *op.cit.* p. 28.

Chez les excellents poètes, il n'y a pas de métaphore, de comparaison ou d'épithète qui ne soit d'une adaptation mathématiquement exacte dans la circonstance actuelle, parce que ces comparaisons, ces métaphores et ces épithètes sont puisées dans l'inépuisable fonds de *l'universelle analogie*, et qu'elles ne peuvent être puisées ailleurs.

A supreme example in the adaptation of the mystical doctrine waits to be discussed—one in which the philosopher himself is absorbed and effaced. Turn, not to one of the last of Baudelaire's writings, but to that section of *Les Paradis Artificiels* called *Le Poème du Haschiche*. Admirably written, more original than the rest, which was mainly adapted from De Quincey, this piece was published in a review in 1858, the year after the appearance of *Les Fleurs du Mal* and two years before it appeared as part of a new work. In an interesting series of paragraphs beginning with a description of the 'homme moderne sensible' (doubtless a sketch of the Baudelairian type) the author proceeds to show what happens to such a sensibility under the effect of hashish:

Si vous êtes une de ces âmes, votre amour inné de la forme et de la couleur trouvera tout d'abord une pâture immense dans les premiers développements de votre ivresse.[1]

The temperament affected is obviously artistic and the intensity imparted by the drug to colour and design is stressed and gracefully illustrated in the sequel. Then comes a plunge into mystical depths, one of the most famous sentences in the poet's prose:

Cependant se développe cet état mystérieux et temporaire de l'esprit, où la profondeur de la vie, hérissée de ses problèmes multiples, se révèle tout entière dans le spectacle, si naturel et si trivial qu'il soit, qu'on a sous les yeux,—où le premier objet venu devient symbole parlant.

[1] *Les Paradis artificiels* (Edition Conard,) p. 50.

Immediately the names of Fourier and Swedenborg occur; but note how curiously their philosophic personalities are transformed by the drug:

> Fourier et Swedenborg, l'un avec ses *analogies*, l'autre avec ses *correspondances*, se sont incarnés dans le végétal et l'animal qui tombent sous votre regard, et, au lieu d'enseigner par la voix, ils vous endoctrinent par la forme et par la couleur.

The condensation here is intense enough to be confusing. But it is clear that the philosophers are made to teach, not through their natural oral media, but through plastic modes of exposition *as if they were artists*, so powerful and personal a wrench has the poet's imagination imposed upon their functions through the intervention of hashish. Actually the drug merely accentuates Baudelaire's fundamental attitude. Enough will have been said to enable us to conclude that what he drew from the various symbolical philosophies with which he was acquainted (and of which his knowledge was intuitive and derived rather than direct and circumstantial) was a conception of poetry and art which was itself symbolical. This in itself would have been sufficient to make him a master for the Symbolists.

POSTSCRIPT

In his essay on Coleridge Swinburne says of *Kubla Khan*, 'In reading it we seem rapt into that paradise revealed to Swedenborg, where music and colour and perfume were one, where you could hear the hues and see the harmonies of heaven'. Swinburne assumes with Baudelaire that Swedenborg had a developed sense of synaesthesia. May he not have derived this notion from the same sources in Balzac's *Livre Mystique*? Having found no trace of the phenomenon in my limited reading of the seer's work, I consulted the authority of Rev. E. A. Sutton, Principal of New Church College, who replied as follows:

I know of no teaching in Swedenborg's works to suggest that he held ideas such as that with which Swinburne credits him. No references in his pre-theological period admit of such a notion, though he treats of the senses fairly fully in *The Five Senses* (Swedenborg Scientific Association, 1914). Nor does anything like 'synaesthesia' seem to characterize Swedenborg's insight into the spiritual world. Indeed, in all such experiences, it would not be his natural senses which would then operate.

He has much to say of the 'common sensory' where, physiologically, all sensations seem to be pooled, but I find no reference to the precise phenomenon of which you write.

I have been present when Miss Helen Keller has analysed the perfume from a bowl of flowers, named the flowers, and even mentioned their colours, but I do not think she would have derived a perception of the colours from the scents. And being a keen reader of Swedenborg she would have known the point to which you refer if he had developed any such notion.

Of Unity, Swedenborg had written a great deal—but it is all so dispersed throughout his theological works. Pott's *Concordance of Swedenborg* quotes nine columns of references (vol. v) in the notes of 'One'. I suggest *Divine Love and Wisdom* (Swedenborg Society and Everyman Library) nos. 14-27; *Divine Providence* (same publishers) nos. 1-9; and *True Christian Religion*, first Chapter in 'God' where Unity, 'One', and the Infinite are dealt with in a general way.

P.S. Swedenborg makes much of the point that *all* senses are refinements of the sense of touch, and thus have a common basis.

C

CHAPTER II

POE, BAUDELAIRE AND MALLARMÉ:
A PROBLEM OF LITERARY JUDGMENT

I

IN 1852, having translated a selection of the tales of Poe, Charles Baudelaire sent a copy of his work to Sainte-Beuve with the injunction: 'Il faut, c'est-à-dire je désire, qu'Edgar Poe, qui n'est pas grand'chose en Amérique, devienne un grand homme pour la France'.[1] In 1874 Mallarmé published a prose translation of *The Raven*, illustrated with five of Manet's drawings. Fourteen years later he dedicated a group of translations from the poems of Poe, including *Le Corbeau*, as 'un monument du goût français au génie qui à l'égal de nos maîtres les plus vénérés, exerça chez nous une influence'. In an essay first published in 1920,[2] the claim that Poe was a 'grand homme' was revived by the most distinguished of Mallarmé's disciples, the late Paul Valéry, who affirmed that Anglo-Saxons alone refuse to accept Poe as a poet. And M. André Fontainas seems to have made a no less partial, if less dignified, protest. 'Why the devil', he asked of an American correspondent, 'won't your fellow-countrymen admit once and for all that Edgar Poe was one of the most wonderful, most *influential* and most profound poets who ever lived?'[3]

As an example of our unregenerate attitude one may cite a

---

[1] *Lettres de Baudelaire* (Paris, 1907), p. 91.

[2] As an introduction to *Les Fleurs du Mal* (Payot); collected in *Variété II: Situation de Baudelaire*.

[3] Quoted from *The Literary Review*, 22 July 1922, by C. P. Cambriaire (see below).

chapter in Mr Aldous Huxley's *Vulgarity in Literature*. There we find exposed most of the artifices and mannerisms which have made it difficult for many of us to retain beyond our school-days much enthusiasm for the author of *The Bells* and *Annabel Lee*. 'The substance of Poe is refined', says Mr Huxley; 'it is his form that is vulgar. He is, as it were, one of Nature's Gentlemen, unhappily cursed with incorrigible bad taste'. Yet a generation or two of refined French poets could accept the practical demonstrations and even the more uncouth contrivances of Poe's taste as part of a technique which they continued seriously to imitate and extol.

The contradiction in attitudes seems insoluble, unless we shift our ground, as Mauclair did, from the poet to the ideologue. We might then tentatively agree on a conclusion of this kind. If the quality of Poe's achievement leaves us in doubt as to whether he was often a good poet or invariably even a successful versifier, the original example set by his tales and the germinating power of many of his notions about the nature and the art of poetry are beyond question. It would be futile to deny the enormous fascination that his tales, his ideas and his 'legend' have exercised even outside France. And though we might still refuse to impute greatness to Poe, we may have to agree with Mauclair when he says from the French standpoint: 'There is an order of feelings and premonitions which hadn't been expressed by us before he came: no more can be said of the greatest.'[1]

In the most judicious book yet written about Poe, Mr Edward Shanks considers it plausible to maintain 'that he was the true parent of that movement which swept over Europe in the latter half of the nineteenth century and which is described sometimes

---

[1] Camille Mauclair, *L'Art en Silence* (Paris, 1901), p. 41.

as the "Decadent", and sometimes as the "Symbolist" movement'.[1] For a quarter of a century, off and on, critics, researchers and thesis-writers have been attempting to trace the ramifications, and to appraise the results, of his extensive influence on modern French literature. Few impressions emerge more clearly from a comparison of most of these works than that of the lack of finality attaching to asseverations based on such exercises in academic investigation. Nor could any academic exercise show more clearly than two or three of them do the folly of entrusting a subject of this scope and subtlety to novices. Or perhaps the folly lies in allowing the results to be published. Among senior investigators one of the first is M. Louis Seylaz, to whose *Edgar Poe et les premiers symbolistes français* (Lausanne, 1923) subsequent students have been indebted.[2] Wider and more exact researches have been made by M. Léon Lemonnier, who has condensed his knowledge of part of the field into a small book called *Edgar Poe et les poètes français*.[3] M. André Ferran's thesis, *L'Esthétique de Baudelaire*,[4] the most comprehensive piece of recent scholarship on the French poet, has a section on the facts and consequences of his relationship to Poe. But in varying degrees all these works deserve the corrective of an admirable revision by M. Régis Michaut with its amply justified 'conseils de

[1] Edward Shanks, *Edgar Allan Poe*, p. 7.

[2] For instance C. P. Cambriaire, *The Influence of E. A. Poe* (New York, 1927). I cannot share the respect Mr Shanks seems to have for this industrious work. M. Seylaz's, though suggestive and informed, leaves much to be desired in precision and sense of evidence.

[3] Editions de la Nouvelle Revue Critique, Paris, 1932. By the same author: *Les Traducteurs d'Edgar Poe* (Paris) and *Edgar Poe et la Critique française* (out of print).

[4] Paris, 1933. Dr Enid Starkie's *Baudelaire* and her recent edition of the *Fleurs du Mal* will be known to English readers. They are happily free from the excesses of the 'influence' craze.

prudence à l'usage des spécialistes de la comparaison littéraire'.[1] His article has a hygienic effect after the gross assumptions and *parti pris* of the source-hunters.

For me the subject has been refreshed by reverting, over the heads of the researchers, to some of the original texts and by attempting an approach along lines other than those used by the *comparatistes*. This has resulted in certain divergencies of emphasis which I think point to shortcomings different in nature from those exposed by M. Michaut. The question I attempt to raise is whether studies of this kind can ever be effectively consummated if they continue to evade the problems of literary judgment and perception which underlie the complex phenomenon of influence between writers whose work has any literary value.

II

To many readers in France Baudelaire has been known as the translator of Poe's tales rather than as the author of *Les Fleurs du Mal*. But it was not by his work of translation that he established the American's reputation as a maligned and tragic genius, a hero of letters, a poet of equable distinction. The foundation for these views was laid in three attractively written essays, through which probably more than by any other channel the influence of Poe's thought and work reached the Symbolists. The first was a serial article, immature and mainly biographical, published in a couple of numbers of the *Revue de Paris* in 1852. Much of this was incorporated in the later essays: an account of the life and work, prefixed to the *Histoires Extraordinaires* of 1856 and the *Notes*

[1] Régis Michaut, 'Baudelaire et Edgar Poe: Une mise au point', *Revue de Littérature Comparée*, Oct.-Dec. 1938. Cf. another golden text: 'La méthode des passages parallèles est mauvaise quand elle reste purement littérale et qu'elle se base sur des indications tendancieuses et des conclusions qui dépassent les prémisses.'

nouvelles sur Edgar Poe, introducing the series of 1857. One of Baudelaire's letters reveals the intention of composing a book on the personality, talent and doctrines of the American, comprising these two notices augmented by a third part, *Dernières notes sur Edgar Poe*, which was never written.

The finished pieces are of considerable length, but they contain no criticism. Except for a few reservations, the tone in which the works are referred to would imply that Baudelaire accepted them as all of exceptional originality and value. He insists on Poe's virtues as a stylist, especially on the purity of his style. The claim that it was 'adequate' may pass. But such a phrase as 'Poe est toujours correct', though used to point a contrast between the unruly imagination and the deliberate control of the writing, holds one up; and hesitation increases as the encomiums multiply. Obviously there is no concern to judge with detachment. The admirer is transported by a mood of impulsive yet sustained appreciation, often intuitive, often erroneous, always assimilative. He is in the situation of the artist who makes more of his model than we can see in it. The model is 'good', because it shows him what he is looking for and how to realize it. And Poe becomes for Baudelaire and through his insistence for two or three generations of French poets, a 'grand homme'.

Equally partial on the expository side, these pieces, by their compassionate eloquence, contributed greatly to the popularity of their subject. Indeed, since the most fruitful of his services have been the translation of the tales and the presentation of the ideas, we may, I think, define Baudelaire's practical devotion to the work of Poe simply as a labour of *haute vulgarisation*.

Much of the first essay is occupied with the story-writer, or rather with the tales, which constitute 'une littérature nouvelle'. The marks of the method are 'conjecturisme' and 'probabilisme', terms which are not defined but illustrated by numerous summaries. Here as elsewhere the writer shows himself impressed with the technical side of Poe's art.

The introduction to the *Histoires Extraordinaires*, almost exclusively biographical, condenses much of what had appeared in the *Revue de Paris*. The usual emphasis on Poe's qualities is effected by contrasting him with his milieu. The exalted tone, the high tension that vitiates the treatment should be noted:

Si vous ajoutez à cette vision impeccable du vrai, véritable infirmité dans de certaines circonstances, une délicatesse exquise de sens qu'une note fausse torturait, une finesse de goût que tout, excepté l'exacte proportion, révoltait, un amour insatiable du Beau, qui avait pris la puissance d'une passion morbide, vous ne vous étonnerez pas que pour un pareil homme la vie soit devenue un enfer, et qu'il ait mal fini; vous admirerez qu'il ait pu *durer* aussi longtemps.

This is mainly a projection of the writer's sensibility and aspiration. Not that the points made are totally inapplicable to the American. The question is one of degree and of unconscious motivation. The delicacy, the finesse implied proceed from a tendency to idealize, we might say to 'sublimate', the *alter ego*. The dignity of the personality is referred to with equal exaggeration. Even his drunkenness has its excuse as a stimulant to genius, a method of work, the refuge of a superior solitary from his compatriots' lack of comprehension, an example, in fact, of 'ivrognerie littéraire'. Admitting that he has little to say about the work of this 'singular genius', Baudelaire concludes with a few more pages of biased, if brilliant, characterization.

Of the three attempts to present the American, the last was by far the most important for the purposes of Symbolism. It is a noble piece of writing, sustained by personal fervour for the general outlook and aesthetic of Poe. The first half is a defence of the social and political attitudes identified with the model and endorses, with acknowledgments to *The Colloquy of Monos and Una*, his aristocratic disdain for the modern heresies of progress, democracy and civilization. Around a few selected texts Baudelaire develops, with a subtlety and warmth all his own, an apology for decadent literature, balancing original sin or radical perversity against inevitable progress and humanitarianism.

In the second half, following the model more closely, he expounds Poe's anti-utilitarian theory of poetry as an autonomous exercise of the spirit. After a couple of paragraphs on his conception of the short story, with a hint at the role in his art of science, method and analysis, Baudelaire concentrates on the *Poetic Principle* and its denunciation of the literary 'heresies' of the long poem and of didacticism, passion, truth or morality, regarded as the poem's *raison d'être*. Poetry is 'an elevating excitement of the Soul—quite independent of that passion which is the intoxication of the Heart—or of that Truth which is the satisfaction of the Reason'. Poetry is an end in itself, or as Baudelaire puts it: 'La vérité n'a rien à faire avec les chansons'.

All this he adopts, recasting it in clear, orderly, elegant paragraphs, drawn from more than one of Poe's writings,[1] but fused into a superior form. The argument rises to a high note, adapted and condensed from his model's most idealistic flight, to which a turn is given not to be found in the original: 'C'est cet admirable, cet immortel instinct du Beau qui nous fait considérer la terre et ses spectacles comme un aperçu, comme une correspondance du Ciel . . .' This use of the word 'correspondance' Baudelaire took from Swedenborg. Despite what most commentators have

---

[1] E.g. a paragraph on the poet, *genus irritabile*, is a literal rendering of one of the *Fifty Suggestions*.

suggested, it is not used by Poe in this sense, although it fits naturally enough into the idealism of his argument. For Baudelaire, Poe was an *illuminé*.

The exponent comes finally to the *Philosophy of Composition*, the explanation of how *The Raven* was composed. The 'extraordinary elevation, exquisite delicacy and accent of immortality', which he finds characteristic of the American's conception of the nature and function of poetry, far from having made him inattentive to execution, had sharpened his genius as a practising artist. In Poe's insistence on the choice of means to produce chosen effects, in his vigilant resistance to abandoning any part of the poet's task to chance, we see the source of that conception which has reigned in France from Baudelaire to Paul Valéry, and by which, in opposition to the romantic conception of spontaneous creation or improvisation, 'inspiration' is exchanged for 'control', the conscious domination and voluntary disposal of the means of art. The uses Poe makes of 're-echoing rhyme', refrain, repetition and 'retours obstinés de phrases' are enumerated with the admission that the value of such suggestive devices depends on the manner of their application. (They will be variously applied by the Symbolists.) Then, after another flattering characterization of Poe's poetry, comes a defence of it against the supporters of 'la morale utile', who are, as often as not, 'les mauvais critiques'.

The partialities of this presentation are obvious, but as propaganda it was effective, establishing the popularity of Poe's aesthetic and example for half a century. For the American presents an acute case of the writer whose influence abroad *is* his reputation. The tales attracted many of the poets who succeeded Baudelaire, some imitating them in their own short stories, others appropriating much from them in theme, technique or atmosphere for their poems and plays. Yet, from the poetic standpoint, these are side-issues compared with the importance of the ideas. The whole aesthetic system of the most influential of modern French poets, says Ferran, was founded on suggestions from *The Poetic Principle*. Verlaine's *Art Poétique* he derives from the same source.[1] And when allowances are made for the wholesale way in which some researchers tend to identify what is most characteristic of one author with the work of a predecessor, that a measure of truth adheres to these assertions is confirmed by the opinion and experience of Paul Valéry, who, from the earliest essays in *Variété I* to the lectures he delivered at the Collège de France before the outbreak of the recent war, reiterated his sense of indebtedness in terms direct or indirect: 'Poe montrait une voie, il enseignait une doctrine très séduisante et très rigoureuse, dans laquelle une sorte de mathématique et une sorte de mystique s'unissaient.'[2]

III

What good fortune, it has been suggested, for Poe to have found his advocate. But was the luck not also Baudelaire's to have discovered the perfect model, the man, the poet, the experimentalist, appropriately distanced and practically unknown, on whom he could project his ideal? The lack of judgment—it was also a lack of knowledge—results in an erroneous impression of constant elevation and equable distinction, qualities in which Poe's

[1] Actually Poe's comparisons of poetry with music as indefinite arts, which closely resemble Verlaine's argument, are to be found not, as Ferran implies, in *The Poetic Principle*, but elsewhere, e.g. *Marginalia*, ccxiv.

[2] *Situation de Baudelaire*. Valéry finds that Baudelaire's work conforms 'remarkably' to the precepts of Poe. But what conformities he notes in *Les Fleurs du Mal* are negative points—lack of anecdote or description, etc.—which distinguish them from the poems of the Romantics.

work is conspicuously deficient. No perception is shown of the characteristic alternations of soaring philosopher and hack writer. For the most serious defect of Baudelaire's presentation is not that it pitches the note too high, but that it gives no hint of realizing that Poe's fluctuations show, in Mr Shanks's words, 'the wildest oscillations between good and bad'.[1]

It is such contrasts in judgment that present the authentic problem in the study of this relationship, the problem they raise being literary and not factual, moral or psychological. To be germinative and effective, it would appear, an influence need not of necessity be based on exact, circumstantial comprehension of an original. It may proceed from a predominantly subjective apprehension, in which the original becomes more or less transformed or denaturalized in the crucible of the admirer's enthusiasm. Mallarmé is said to have 'corrected' the vision of Baudelaire. This, I think, is doubtful. Verlaine was certainly nearer than either in artistic temper to Poe. But for them as for a hundred other French writers, the conception of the American and his work has for almost a century differed radically from the general reaction and estimate common in England and America. If ever finality is to be reached in this matter, is it likely to come by ignoring this divergence?

Baudelaire, as d'Aurevilly put it, 'translated Poe twice, in his works and in his life, although the latter wasn't comparable'. Allowances must be made, since the biographical material on which he drew was limited and prejudiced. His abhorrence of Griswold, the 'vampire-pedagogue', may have made him partial to the generous impressions left by Poe's few friends. His exaggeration of unpropitious circumstances into a 'special anathema', against which the luckless writer was thought incessantly

[1] *Op. cit.* p. 8.

to have struggled, turns the relapsing inebriate, whom some people were eager to help, into a hero with the world against him. The belief in his 'vast learning', his 'knowledge of several tongues', his 'haute distinction naturelle' are equally wide of the mark. But these misconceptions are explicable on a basis of ascertainable fact, access to which was impossible to Baudelaire. What so far has not been explained—and it cannot be explained on such a basis—is how a critic of Baudelaire's penetration could have acclaimed Poe as a perfect artist and a man of refined taste. For this kind of estimate he had not to rely on hearsay or comment; the works were in his hands and he had translated many of them.

Of this problem none of the researchers show themselves aware. Ferran insists that Baudelaire, after daily contact with the work of Poe, had come to re-live it in his own experience to the point of identifying its author with himself even more perhaps than he identified himself with its author. From the first he applied tastes, attitudes and aspirations to the object of his admiration which were far more characteristically his own. Although induced by arguments found in the American's writings to exchange his early democratic leanings for an attitude of aristo-cratic aloofness, the Frenchman endowed the American with a 'dandyism', an affectation of Satanic revolt, which was part of his own mode of life and thought, but which had never belonged to the man he admired. The sinister Poe who might have escaped from a novel by Sue, the romantic fallen angel, the saturnine poet, the macabre inebriate—these, he says, constitute the figure of a legend.[1]

But Ferran is almost exclusively concerned with the moral and ideological aspects of what he calls this case of 'co-penetration'.

[1] *Op. cit.* p. 202.

That Baudelaire transforms Poe into a literary model by enhancing his qualities and endowing him, here too, with qualities of his own; that his presentation rests on a misconception of, or an indifference to, the intrinsic value of Poe's work, which is un-consciously assimilated to the Frenchman's standards and achievements—this aspect of the phenomenon has not received sufficient attention, if any at all. Ferran contrasts Baudelaire's conception of Poe, the man, with the reality; Baudelaire's estimate of the poet and writer he makes no attempt to compare with the poet and writer Poe actually was.

The root of the French poet's misrepresentation was not in having conceived of the American as 'un jeune gentleman de génie, vaquant quelquefois à la littérature au milieu de mille occupations d'une vie élégante'; he had already seen his mistake, when he used the words.[1] His important error was to acclaim Poe as an 'aristocratic' artist, the type who dominates his work, who invariably strives to produce work perfectly finished ac-cording to self-imposed standards. Baudelaire strove to live up to this ideal. The reverse is true of Poe. He preached the doctrine of control in tones that were to find echoes in France for a century; but he cannot be said to have practised it with any consistency, except perhaps for the length of a tale. 'He was not by temper a meticulous artist', says Mr Middleton Murry in the most favourable account of his poetry I have read.[2] On Poe's abundant lapses of taste, his very frequent depressions, Baudelaire is silent; though the American was not unaware of them. 'In de-fence of my own taste', he wrote in the preface to the 1849 edition of the poems, 'it is incumbent upon me to say that I think nothing

---

[1] In *Le Pays*, 25 July 1854. See *Histoires Extraordinaires* (Edition Conard), p. 391.

[2] *Discoveries: Poe's Poetry*.

in this volume of much value to the public or very creditable to myself'. But what Poe may have felt is not to the point. It is with the impression his French admirers give of him as an artist that we are here concerned, and with the contrast between that and the impression his work as a whole makes on us. The problem of influence has become a problem of literary judgment.

IV

To his American public Poe was fond of presenting himself as an arbiter of taste, a role he attempted to fill seriously. That he was perpetually concerned with problems of taste is evident from his critical and theoretical writings; and it is possible that he achieved more than has been recorded by dinning them into the ears of his countrymen. But when it comes to his own taste as reflected in his work, whether or not we should wish to decorate rooms according to a scheme based on the *Philosophy of Furniture* or regard *Landor's Cottage* as a model of appropriate design, what nowadays seems to admit of little doubt is that English readers do not—with some notable exceptions—think highly of Poe's verse; approval, at best, is shown for very little of it.

Finely appreciative points have been made about some of the poems by Mr Walter de la Mare. 'Concerning no man of genius or of fudge', he says, 'are the critics even of our own days more acridly at odds.'[1] But the unflattering alternative, which is repeated in another context, seems to indicate a sense of damaging inequalities. Apart from the selected favourite, *To Helen*, which Mr Shanks describes as 'the best poem so uncharacteristic of its author that ever was written',[2] which Lowell thought fit for the Greek Anthology and which for Baudelaire seems to have been

---

[1] *Early One Morning*, pp. 246-7.   [2] *Op. cit.* p. 88.

no more than an immature pastiche, the better pieces are rarely exhibited. Mr Murry and Mr Shanks have praised certain fragments and short poems like *Romance, The Sleeper, Israfel*, and Mr de la Mare points to that remarkable juvenile song—

The bower whereat in dreams I see . . . .

In these the characteristic mannerisms are subtly disposed, not hammered home as in those that have made Poe's reputation: *The Raven, The Bells, Annabel Lee, For Annie*. They are pronounced even in *Ulalume*, to the influence of which Mr Shanks attaches singular importance.

Emerson called Poe the 'jingle-man'; and there is a kind of pathos in the fact that, having written so much about his art— on tone, appropriateness, effect, rhyme, rhythm, alliteration, refrains and repetitive devices—he should have produced to illustrate his theories some of the vulgarest tintinnabulations in English verse, as 'grim, ungainly, ghastly, gaunt' as the reappearances of his ominous bird, providing patterns of clamorous doggerel for schoolboys to parody or light-versifiers to emulate for their heavier blows. Is there not something of a literary curiosity in the fact that certain French poets—reputed to rank with the most exquisite of their race—should have troubled to adapt so many of Poe's tricks and tags to their purposes, producing, even when crudities are softened, effects which appear to be no more in keeping with the French tradition than their prototypes were with the English? 'Poe's care for technique', says Mr Shanks, 'became an inflammation.'[1] The excitement over it in France raged around the more 'inflamed' pieces of artifice. Those that receive honourable mention from Baudelaire are *The Bells*—

---

[1] *Op. cit.* p. 175. The French admirers are not alone in their attitude to Poe's technique. Mr Shanks reminds us of the equally ecstatic admiration of John Davidson.

'une véritable curiosité littéraire'—*The Raven, Dreamland, Ulalume, Annabel Lee*; and what the successors of Baudelaire imitate are precisely the more mechanical mannerisms. From him to the last of the Symbolists and from the first to the latest French investigator of the influence, the reiterated praise or the implied approval of Poe's style and technique—especially the recommendation of his 'complicated rhythms'—seems completely to miss both the 'something meretricious' detected in the poems by an admirer like Arthur Symons and the defects that D. H. Lawrence exposed in *Studies in Classical American Literature*:

All Poe's style has this mechanical quality as his poetry has a mechanical rhythm. He never sees anything in terms of life, almost always in terms of matter, jewels, marbles, etc.—or in terms of force, scientific. And his cadences are all managed mechanically. That is what is called 'having style'.

The difficulty of appreciating the effects of technical innovation in a foreign medium is formidable. It is obvious that Poe's French admirers could not have felt the defects and excesses of his manner as we do.[1] The American was a restless experimenter, providing patterns which, transplanted in the poetic soil of late nineteenth-century France, produced, along with a crop of flat, unassimilated pastiches, a few repetitive varieties which, manipulated by the delicate touch of a Verlaine, are not without charm.

[1] Contrast with Lawrence's judgment this apology made in 1864 by Armand Renaud on behalf of the 'effets produits par les répétitions': 'Il en résulte de cette agglomération de sons semblables une sorte de monotonie, mais monotonie tellement artistique qu'au lieu de causer l'ennui, cela devient quelque chose d'étrange qui fascine et qui berce. . . .La forme matérielle de la poésie d'Edgar Poe répond précisément à la forme de ses idées; avec d'autres poètes, ce serait puéril et prétentieux, avec lui c'est magique.' Cited by Lemonnier, *op. cit.* p. 66. The same superstition or obtuseness about Poe's value as a technician runs through the whole French tradition of imitation and research, including M. Lemonnier himself.

On the whole, however, the effects of this craze were disastrous.

This view is, of course, subject to the reservations we have just made. Nothing could better illustrate the difficulty of dealing with an influence between writers in different languages than the realization that, to be effective, the judgment must operate at ease, and with equal assurance in the foreign as well as in the native literature. The best results might perhaps be obtained by the co-operation of two critical minds representing the nationalities of the writers under consideration. All that can be said in support of our own view is that the cruder imitations, such as many of those practised by Henri de Régnier, strike us as totally out of keeping with the tradition of French poetical expression, and, more objectively, that such experiments have had no sequel. They remain, if ever they are recalled, the eccentric monopoly of the more degenerate of the Decadents, who were, in fact, the direct progeny of the *engouement* for Poe.

But as a model Poe's poetry has more intimate disqualifications than the crudities of its technique. Of his slender output, much hovers between sentimentality and melodrama. Much is immature in conception and facile in execution. For Mr Shanks its effect is 'blurred'. How then could Baudelaire and, forty years later, Mallarmé reach and reiterate their conviction of its 'crystal' quality, its *purity*? That is perhaps the most intriguing aspect of the whole problem: it raises the question, not of the *notion* of 'pure poetry' derived from *The Poetic Principle*, but of the *example* of 'purity' found in the poems themselves. With the best of Blake and Coleridge in mind, can we be expected to think of Poe as the exemplar of the pure poet?

Most of us do not, and the injustice, if it is one, must, I think, be due to his inequalities. For he wrote a few poems in which, taken as wholes or in parts, the quintessence has been detected even by some of his most severe critics. The precious nucleus is restricted enough and its constituents would probably be composed somewhat differently by people of differing tastes. Yet, what is important is not to decide how we should pick and choose, but to realize that there were, after all, intelligible reasons for the French recognition of Poe's peculiar merits as a poet— if only they had not been exaggerated!

Baudelaire's final appreciation of his poetry in the *Notes nouvelles* throws light on this point. Its 'powerful effect' he distinguishes from both the ardent effusion of Byron and the harmonious melancholy of Tennyson: 'C'est quelque chose de profond et de miroitant comme le rêve, de mystérieux et de parfait comme le crystal.' His earlier characterizations had erred in assimilating the poems he admired to his own plastic conceptions. Here he has found a formula which is applicable, by no means to all Poe's poems, several of which he misjudged, but to the finer residue; though here again he makes no distinctions. All were 'equally interesting', as he told Vigny.

Baudelaire's dominant attitude is epitomized in Mallarmé's. The claim that the latter's estimate was more acute can scarcely survive an examination of the notes and '*scolies*' which accompany his renderings of most of the poems.[1] He admirably hits off Baudelaire's presentation of the personality as 'le suprême tableau à la Delacroix, moitié réel et moitié moral'. But although he scents the exaggeration and suggests that Poe had led the simple and monotonous existence of a man of letters in a country where such a condition was above all a craft, he too joins in the adulation of the poet. If he excludes a few pieces, it is to present only the

---

[1] *Les Poèmes d'Edgar Poe, traduction de Stéphane Mallarmé, avec portrait et fleuron par Edouard Manet.* A Bruxelles chez l'éditeur Edmond Deman, 1888.

'marvels'. He pitches the tone even higher, capping the insistence on 'purity' with the claim that almost each one of a group of twenty pieces is a 'chef-d'œuvre unique'.

But although he participates in the reverential cult, Mallarmé has taken up the challenge implied in his predecessor's conviction that the dream of translating the poems must remain a dream. Profoundly impressed by the task, he presents his versions as an unpretentious *calque*, aimed at rendering what he calls 'quelques-uns des effets de sonorité extraordinaire de la musique originelle et ici et là peut-être le sentiment même'. His notes on the poems deal admittedly with external aspects of their conception or execution and he definitely eschews the critic's task. Many of the points he makes derive from his correspondence with American friends of Poe like Sarah Helen Whitman; and his famous sonnet on Poe is included with translations by Mrs Whitman and another American poetess.

It has been said that Mallarmé's renderings soften the crudities of the originals, and for us they do. But Poe's mannerisms must have been anything but crude for an admirer who could call Annabel Lee 'l'héroïne au nom chantant' and could point to the 'strange alliterative effects' of—

And the yellow-haired young Eulaly [*sic*] became my . . . .

As for his attempt to turn *The Bells*—the only one 'really untranslatable', 'a demon for the translator'—Mallarmé fears that its 'richesse impalpable' (!) will be entirely lost in the operation. *For Annie* inspires a single venture in judgment: 'je dirais que la poésie de Poe n'est peut-être jamais autant allée hors de tout ce que nous savons, d'un rythme apaisé et lointain, que dans ce chant.' *For Annie* may be a 'poetic miracle', but it is surely unequal:

And ah! let it never
    Be foolishly said
That my room it is gloomy,
    And narrow my bed;
For man never slept
    In a different bed—
And, to *sleep*, you must slumber
    In just such a bed.

In concluding I suggest that the obliviousness to Poe's im-
perfections, which is the most curious feature in the hallucinated
attitude of these most critical minds, may be regarded as the
result of a confusion of two interrelated but not identical ideals—
the idea of the Pure and the idea of the Perfect. The French
tradition is dominated by the idea of the Perfect, which becomes
inextricably involved for the poets we are considering in their
notion of poetic purity. But the cult of perfection in its modern
phase belongs to the Gautier-Baudelaire-Flaubert tradition,
coming to its most exigent consciousness in Mallarmé, 'martyr de
l'idée du parfait', as his disciple Valéry called him. In origin it is a
plastic-Parnassian conception; it has nothing to do with E. A. Poe.
His French admirers, however, obsessed with their traditional
ideal and unconsciously fusing it with the notion of purity,
developed with many elaborations and subtleties from the simple
formulae of *The Poetic Principle*, have persistently read it back
into Poe's work. Thus his poetry has for Baudelaire 'quelque
chose de *parfait* comme le *crystal*'; while for Mallarmé it is 'pur
comme le *diamant*'. This retains the notion of the pure, omitted
from Baudelaire's final characterization, but assimilates it, as
indeed Baudelaire had always done, to one of the accepted symbols
of plastic perfection, the jewel, the crystal, the diamond. What is
wrong with the whole series of judgments is not so much the
perception of purity, which is present, as Mr Spender recently

admitted, in 'one or two' of Poe's poems; what is wrong is the persistent implication that Poe is one of the perfect artists.

This may be allowed without depreciating all the consequences of the cult. It seems probable that Baudelaire and his successors apprehended the ethereal qualities of English Romanticism through a few of the poems of Poe. Why, we might ask, did they not become equally excited about Coleridge, Shelley or Keats? Part of the answer, no doubt, would be that none of these had written tales of mystery and imagination. Only De Quincey could compete with Poe in that sense and De Quincey's essays were too personal, too inimitable to take on with anyone but Baudelaire himself. The answer, too, would involve the peculiar tragedy of Poe's life, which Baudelaire and several of the Decadents could tolerably well assimilate to their own. In another point the French estimate was still less mistaken. What Poe had preached he applied: all his poems are free from the extraneous elements he had condemned. Even when entangled in a rhetoric of their own, they are innocent of eloquence.

Yet what appealed to the French poets was probably far less the rare examples of Poe's lyrical quality, glimpsed more often than not through translations that were beginning to multiply, than his theoretic persistence in emphasizing the autonomy of Beauty and his perception of the untrammelled realization of the Poetic Sentiment in music and in poetry conceived as music. It is here we touch the 'greatness' of Poe, in the inerrancy of his premonitions for poetry as well as in his generous effort to defend poetry as an exercise of the spirit operating on the plane of the ideal, to adapt such a defence to a popular level and to formulate it in the teeth of the moralizing vindictiveness of native hacks and hypocrites. The experiment was effective. Its success almost persuaded the lecturer to return to Richmond, where he had lived. Yet the response, if consoling, was parochial; it could have given him no inkling of the extraordinary reception that awaited his ideas abroad, once he had shuffled off. The Symbolist movement of 1885 was inspired by a mood not dissimilar to that in which the ill-starred journalist had put together his incongruous notions for the lecture at Richmond—a mood of revolt against the materialism, the utilitarianism, the inveterate ethical rhetoric of nineteenth-century bourgeois mentality, a revolt too against official Romanticism, 'la poésie facile', the poetry of comfortable ideas, which fostered and flattered that mentality.

CHAPTER III

POE AND BAUDELAIRE: THE 'AFFINITY'

SOME of the more industrious researchers have attempted to clear up the confusions that have obscured the chronology of Poe's penetration into France. They are not themselves in complete agreement; but the following facts seem established. Poe's reputation had to emerge from a shadow of vulgarity, his name having been popularized through a somewhat notorious affair. On 12 October 1846 a certain E. D. Forgues, alias Old Nick, published in a paper called *Le Commerce* a much abridged version of *The Murders in the Rue Morgue*, a more complete, though disfigured, translation having appeared earlier in the year in another journal. Neither of these renderings admitted the authorship of the tale, and accusations of plagiarism ensued which led to a lawsuit. In the course of it the counsel for the defence dropped a prophetic hint: 'Grâce à M. Forgues, tout le monde va savoir que M. E. Poe fait des contes en Amérique.' Already in 1845 an adaptation of *The Purloined Letter* had appeared anonymously. Later in the year another of the tales had been translated and published in *La Revue Britannique* with an editorial note which mentioned the author's name for the first time; and a few months before his trial Forgues sent the first article in French on Poe to the *Revue des Deux Mondes* (15 October 1846). From then on Poe's fortunes in France show a decided improvement in quality.

On 27 January 1847 Charles Baudelaire opened *La Démocratie pacifique* and read *Le Chat noir*, one of the tales of Poe turned into

French by Mlle Isabelle Meunier, who translated others for the same journal. His enthusiasm was immediate and unbounded. In a letter to Armand Fraisse, written about ten years later, he describes the circumstances of the discovery in words from which I shall quote later in the original:

I can reveal to you something still more singular, something incredible. In 1846 or '47 I came across a few fragments of Edgar Poe and was strangely disturbed. His complete works not having been collected . . . I had the patience to link up with Americans living in Paris so as to borrow files of the newspapers Poe had directed. It was then I found, believe me if you will, poems and short stories which I had had in my mind, but in a vague, confused, disorderly state, and which Poe had been able to bring off and carry to perfection.

The domination of Baudelaire's mind by this contact was for a time nothing short of spectacular. 'J'ai vu peu de possessions aussi complètes, aussi rapides, aussi absolues', wrote Asselineau. 'Baudelaire', wrote Champfleury, 'pendant de longues années, s'incarna dans Poe'.

He decides to translate the tales and devotes four years to preparation, reading, consulting, brushing up his English and attempting to get into closer touch with his author's mind; not omitting to give offence by impulsive interrogation of travellers, lackeys, waiters, anyone who might be suspected of knowing something about America and whom he accosts, detains and argues with at unconventional moments. He procures every piece of Poe's work he can lay hands on, sets himself the task of translating one tale a day, and rages over the proofs.

On the development of the short story in France the tales have apparently had an enormous effect, and it was Baudelaire who made the best, if not always the first, version. He began with

Mesmeric Revelation, which he translated for *La Liberté de Penser* (15 July 1848). From 1852 for a number of years he regularly sent renderings to the reviews. His version of Poe's most popular poem, *The Raven*, came out in *L'Artiste* (1 March 1853). A few months later the appearance of a thin volume, *Nouvelles choisies d'Edgar Poe*, by another hand, may have urged him to collect his own. A first series, produced in 1856 as the *Histoires Extraordinaires*, was followed in 1857 by the *Nouvelles Histoires Extraordinaires*. *Les Aventures d'A.-G. Pym* appeared *en feuilleton* that year and as a book the next. *Eureka*, part of which had already been published, came out in 1863 and was followed in 1865 by the last of the series, *Les Histoires Grotesques et Sérieuses*. Despite the efforts of many 'rivals', Baudelaire's versions have retained their rank as the most complete and widely diffused; though they are no longer regarded as 'one of the most accurate and brilliant translations in literature'.[1] They represent a serious amount of work and reveal an unexpected degree of persistent application.

The 'influence' begins in a discovery and is sustained by an attraction. Commentators are content to predicate an 'affinity' between the two poets, or rather between their minds; for only a few traces of demonstrable influence have been found in the *Fleurs du Mal*. The assumption is inevitable. But the affinity is the crux of the matter and remains an obscure point. Baudelaire himself throws little light on its intimate nature and the investigators accept it without analysis or argument as the most 'remarkable', the 'unique' case of its kind; or they shroud it in rhetoric. 'Poe', says M. Seylaz, 'fut comme le Messie littéraire qui

---

[1] *Encylopædia Britannica* (9th ed.). It is unfortunate that the one positive note struck in this piece of critical hauteur should have been wide of the mark.

révéla Baudelaire à soi-même'; and M. John Charpentier, who is sometimes acute, can write: 'La "commotion singulière" qu'il dit avoir ressentie au contact du Conteur américain n'est comparable qu'à celle de la grâce pour le chrétien en proie aux affres du doute.'[1] Generally it is agreed that the discovery of Poe helped Baudelaire, not in the popular sense to 'discover his genius', but to realize some of his characteristic faculties and potential *procédés*. The work of the American may, as Charpentier suggests, have replied to most of the questions the French poet set out to solve.

But what has Baudelaire himself to say about a relationship that meant so much to him? He insists on two points which he repeats without elaboration. The first is that he *understands* Poe and has written about him in a mood of sympathetic excitement, illuminated by similar circumstances and sufferings.

J'ai trouvé un auteur américain [he writes to his mother] qui a excité en moi une incroyable sympathie, et j'ai écrit deux articles sur sa vie et ses ouvrages. C'est écrit avec ardeur; mais tu y découvriras sans doute quelques signes d'une très extraordinaire surexcitation. C'est la conséquence de la vie douloureuse et folle que je mène.[2]

Along with this emphasis on his sympathy, his letters show a conviction of *resemblance*. It is worth glancing at the context in which he uses the word. Most of his comments on Poe's work and gifts will be found to refer to the tales and the theories; relatively few refer to the poems. Even when he talks of resemblances between himself and the American, the implication is the

[1] In the course of a somewhat laborious article, 'La poésie britannique et Baudelaire', *Mercure de France*, 15 April and 1 May 1921.

[2] Letter to Mme Baudelaire, 27 March 1852. Cf. 'Comprends-tu maintenant pourquoi, au milieu de l'affreuse solitude qui m'environne, j'ai si bien compris le génie d'Edgar Poe, et pourquoi j'ai si bien écrit son abominable vie?' (26 March 1853).

same. Yet he made one or two unmistakable references to similarities between his poems and Poe's.

The most emphatic is a phrase in the letter from which we have just quoted; it accompanied a copy of Poe's poems. Except for the early pieces and the *Scenes from Politian*, he tells his mother, 'tu ne trouveras que du beau et de l'étrange . . .' Then he adds:

Ce qu'il y a d'assez singulier, et ce qu'il m'est impossible de ne pas remarquer, c'est la ressemblance intime, quoique non positive-ment accentuée, entre mes poésies propres et celles de cet homme, déduction faite du tempérament et du climat.

The feeling of resemblance is for Baudelaire inescapable. But, intimate and independent of temperament and milieu, it is not revealed by positive signs. This is not very helpful, least of all to the type of researcher who conceives the quest of 'influence' as the collection and cataloguing of 'positive signs'. The letter may furnish a faint clue in the association of the words 'beau' and 'étrange'. They fit the *Fleurs du Mal* as they do everything Poe wrote. The American was fond of quoting Bacon's phrase: 'There is no Excellent Beauty, that hath not some Strangeness in the Proportion.' 'Étrangeté', echoes Baudelaire, 'condiment indis-pensable de toute beauté.' He admits differences of temperament. But both he and Poe were involved in that conflict of spiritual extremes, that violent contrast of moods, which he called 'Spleen et Idéal', the pull of a world of evil, hardship, deception, ennui, exerted upon the aspirations of the spirit—'l'extase de la vie et l'horreur de la vie'. The sense of this radical, psychological ambivalence, reflected in the antitheses of their poetry, must, I think, have been one of the chief elements in the French poet's conviction of 'resemblance'.

The statement in the letter to Mme Baudelaire is unique in its definiteness. The much-quoted phrase in the letter to Fraisse, where, referring to his shock of recognition, Baudelaire says he found 'des poèmes et des nouvelles dont j'avais eu la pensée mais vague et confuse, mal ordonnée, et que Poe avait su combiner et mener à la perfection', is on the other hand indefinite, so far as his own achievement goes. Baudelaire wrote no tales after *La Fanfarlo*, though many were planned in imitation of those he was translating. Nor has one any reason for thinking that those 'poems', which vaguely hovered in his mind when he discovered Poe's, were ever written down.

The only other reference worth noting occurs in a letter to Thoré (about 1866). Protesting against the accusation that he imitates the American, the French poet asks: 'Do you know why I so patiently translated Poe?' and retorts:

Parce qu'il me ressemblait. La première fois que j'ai ouvert un livre de lui, j'ai vu avec épouvante et ravissement non seulement des sujets rêvés par moi mais des PHRASES pensées par moi et écrites par lui vingt ans auparavant.

Here the reference is obviously to the tales.

The excuse for bringing these texts together is the difficulty one has in perceiving much, if any, resemblance between the poems of Baudelaire and those of Poe. And the question arises, with what degree of exactitude was the word used? M. Michaut points out that the Frenchman used it of his feelings not only for Poe but also for Delacroix, Wagner, De Quincey and others.[1] Two conclusions, however, seem valid: that his sense of affinity with Poe was stimulated by a belief in similar misfortunes and that its strongest pull operated through the tales and the ideas

[1] R. Michaut, *loc. cit.* The similarity between the phrase in the letter to Thoré and one in a letter Baudelaire had written to Wagner (17 February 1860) is striking enough to suggest that his enthusiasms might prompt the same kind of self-appropriating formula as a supreme compliment to the work of any artist he admired.

rather than through the poems; or between the mind reflected in the tales and ideas and that of the man who translated or adapted them. Charpentier is probably right when he says: 'Baudelaire ne laisse pas de s'illusionner en partie sur l'exactitude de sa ressemblance avec Poe.' Not that he neglected the poems. Ferran makes the surprising statement that Baudelaire seems not to have been particularly struck by the verse of Poe and recalls a reservation he made to Lowell's praise of the shorter piece *To Helen*. Granting that this reflects on the poem itself, I can find only one other reference out of several which is not emphatically flattering —the reservation about the juvenilia in the letter to his mother. In 1854 he called Poe 'un des plus grands poètes de ce temps', and the phrase, 'Sa poésie, profonde et plaintive, est néanmoins ouvragée, pure, correcte et brillante comme un bijou de crystal', published in 1852, reappears with a slight alteration four years later and again with a more significant change in 1857. As late as 1862 he sent Alfred de Vigny a volume of his beloved poet's work with the remark: 'Enfin voici les poésies de Poe. Je ne vous recommande rien, tout est également intéressant.'

And yet what interest Baudelaire took in the poems cannot be compared with his practical preoccupation with the tales. He brought out a rendering of *The Raven* in 1853 and again in 1854, and thought for a time of publishing translations from the poems along with one or other of his selections from the tales. But he advanced no further with this project beyond translating *The Haunted House* as part of *The Fall of the House of Usher* and turning a sonnet Poe had written to Maria Clemm into a dedication for the *Histoires Extraordinaires*.

Passing from the mysteries of affinity to the assumptions of influence, Seylaz makes the biggest claims. He believes that the poems of Baudelaire abound in reminiscences of the tales he was translating. But few of his *rapprochements* convincingly support this view, and he admits that the influence is much more clearly visible in the doctrine of Baudelaire.[1] The superior importance for the latter of Poe's ideas on the nature of poetry and the poet's craft, though frequently stressed—Valéry's essay is largely devoted to them—has not yet been studied in all its literary implications. With this aspect of the relationship I have attempted to deal, though without pretending to any kind of finality in a field that appears to bristle with unsuspected difficulties. As for the relation of the *Fleurs du Mal* to the poems of Poe, some investigators take a dogmatic stand on the dates 1843–4, the pertinent fact being Ernest Prarond's claim that in 1843 he saw in a finished state fifteen of the pieces that went to make up the volume of 1857. Ferran dismisses the point with a vague appeal to the dates.[2] Crépet, in his notes to the Conard edition of the *Fleurs du Mal*, admits that most of the poems must have been composed between 1840 and 1850, but reminds us that they were constantly revised almost up to the poet's death in 1867. And Lemonnier contends that in the process occasional points and turns were incorporated from Poe and other poets of the English tongue. Lemonnier's information is formidable; but he seems to have stretched 'proof' beyond evidence in making an exception of a group of poems, the immediate inspiration of which was a 'platonic' passion for Mme Sabatier, who presided over a salon which attracted Baudelaire in the early fifties. The admirer's attitude to 'La Présidente' is compared with that of Poe to Mrs Whitman and, on the basis of an unimpressive argument, Lemonnier asserts that the poems in question 'clearly' proceed from Poe. The only example he refers to is a sonnet, *Le Flambeau vivant*, which he calls a

[1] L. Seylaz, *Edgar Poe et les premiers symbolistes français*, p. 73.
[2] A. Ferran, *L'Esthétique de Baudelaire*, p. 175.

'paraphrase' of Poe's longer piece *To Helen*, and which Mallarmé unaccountably thought 'admirable'.[1] Actually the French poem rehashes the imagery of the last paragraph of its model, an inferior production of about sixty lines. Of her eyes Poe writes:

> They are my ministers—yet I their slave.
> Their office is to illumine and enkindle—
> My duty, *to be saved* by their bright light . . .
>   unextinguished by the sun!

Baudelaire writes:

> Ils sont mes serviteurs et je suis leur esclave,
> Tout mon être obéit à ce vivant flambeau.
>
>   *   *   *
>
> Astres dont nul soleil ne peut flétrir la flamme!

This and a few more images and phrases are obvious appropriations.[2] It has been claimed that Baudelaire's technique shows signs of the imitation of Poësque modes of repetition, alliteration and internal rhyme. Michaut suggests other and more probable sources for these effects. In any case an assumption of serious influence can hardly be equated with so meagre a handful of details. What usually results from a sensitive comparison of the French with the American poems is a feeling of *difference*. The profound difference between the 'iniquitous' passion of the *Fleurs*

---

[1] I suggest that whenever Poe is directly imitated, whether by Baudelaire or by any other French poet, the closer the imitation the worse the result. Translation is another matter. Lemonnier's argument seems largely invalidated by some recent revelations made in the course of M. Albert Feuillerat's precise and charming study: *Baudelaire et la Belle aux cheveux d'or* (1941), pp. 27, 28.

[2] For details see L. Lemonnier, *Edgar Poe et les poètes français*, pp. 25-32. Actually Baudelaire may have been more indebted to certain minor Romanticists like Philotée O'Neddy and Pétrus Borel. See the valuable notes in Dr Enid Starkie's edition of *Les Fleurs du Mal* (1943), and her article in the *Modern Language Review* for October 1944.

du Mal and the chaste inspirations of the American had been indicated by Huysmans in *A Rebours* as early as 1884. Since then nothing more effective has been written on this aspect than certain paragraphs in Charpentier's article, where some fine distinctions are drawn between the poets. Of the poems of Poe, he says, it was the spirit more than the letter that impressed Baudelaire. If that is true, it is the kind of influence that seems to have evaded the toils of the comparative method.

CHAPTER IV

WHITMAN AND THE SYMBOLISTS

I

FEW tasks could appear more futile than an attempt to compare work so dissimilar as Whitman's *Leaves of Grass* and the poetry of the Symbolists. For what could be further removed from the fastidious sophistication, the oblique allusiveness, the esoteric concealment practised, with varying degrees of subtlety and success, by the French poets of the 'eighties than the rhapsodies and declamations of the 'orbic bard', his exhaustive catalogue of 'materials', his demagogic message, his 'barbaric yawp'? Whitman, though he lived until 1892, probably knew nothing of the experiments of his later contemporaries in France and could hardly be expected to have approved of them. Nor are there reasons for thinking that any effective interaction occurred between him and the leaders of the French movement. The full appeal of his example could not have been felt until the appearance of Léon Bazalgette's complete version in 1909, and by then Symbolism as a movement was spent. Long before that, however, some of his own experiments had been associated with those of the French poets—mainly in the matter of form—and in such a way as to suggest possibilities of an influence. Something in fact of the *Leaves* and their author had been known in France since the 'seventies; and we shall begin with a glance at a few of the articles inspired by Whitman's poetry and reputation and at some of the early translations made from his work, before any question of influence had arisen.[1]

By coincidence, apparently, in 1872 two important reviews dealt almost simultaneously with the new phenomenon. The *Revue des Deux Mondes* for 1 June published an article by Mme Thérèse Bentzon on 'Un poète américain, Walt Whitman'. Headed by the words, 'Muscle and pluck for ever!' it stressed the 'monstrosities' of his manner, making him out to be an incorrigible materialist and showing a complete misunderstanding of his ethics. It abounds in lengthy renderings designed to give an idea of his form and style, the defects of which the author rejoices she is unable to reproduce. She cannot deny his work 'une certaine grandeur et beaucoup de passion', but her attempts to do justice to the man are paralysed by doubts about his healthiness of mind.

A week after this unpropitious introduction another article on Whitman appeared in the seventh number of the *Renaissance artistique et littéraire*, a journal to which Émile Blémont, one of the minor Parnassians, was contributing a series on poetry in England and the United States. Blémont's article ranks with the warmest of early foreign tributes to a poet who, unlike Longfellow, Bryant and Poe, is felt to be 'absolument, essentiellement américain'. Insisting that his subject is quite unknown in France, the writer gives a short biography of the 'pur Yankee' and concludes the first instalment with a summary of Whitman's preface of 1855. The second instalment comes in the eleventh number. Whitman is no versifier; indeed he has few artistic preoccupations. Blémont's enthusiasm cannot blind him to the defects of Whitman's

[1] Here I shall refer only to the more significant of these early notices. More details will be found in an article published in the *Modern Language Review* for January 1915, which is the nucleus of the present study.

style. But if the poet's faults are monstrous, it is because he is a giant: 'S'il n'est pas l'art, il est bien plus, il est la vie.' The essay is concluded in the next number with descriptions of the longer poems and extensive quotations.

Mme Bentzon's article in the *Revue des Deux Mondes* was probably read widely. Blémont's appreciation, written for a much less influential periodical, passed almost unnoticed. Oddly enough, on the other side of the Atlantic, the poet, to whom a friend translated parts of the less favourable article, expressed joy and gratitude for what he took to be homage paid to his work by French thought.

Twelve years seem to have elapsed before anything commensurate with these notices appeared in France. Then, in February 1884, the *Revue politique et littéraire* published a comprehensive essay on Whitman by Léo Quesnel. The author feels that qualities foreign to the French genius must account for the fact that his work remains unknown in France, 'où son nom seul a frappé les oreilles'. Whitman is not enough of an artist to appeal to the writer's countrymen. 'Ses vers pour nous ne sont pas des vers.' The *Leaves* are poetic prose, if you will, but have nothing in common with the art of versification. Yet there are indications that the poetry of the future will lay more stress on matter than on form, and that form will become more amorphous, more suitable to the multifarious variety of modern subjects. In that case Whitman would not be wrong in considering himself 'l'initiateur d'une poétique nouvelle faite à la taille des destinées incommensurables de l'Amérique, un Christophe Colomb de la littérature'. The author declares that the *Leaves* are untranslatable; his one quotation is given in the original with a free rendering below.

The most adequate of these early appreciations appeared in *La*

Nouvelle Revue for 1 May 1888. It was written by Gabriel Sarrazin after the publication of fresh editions of *Leaves of Grass* and *Specimen Days*. Not content with giving a *causerie* on a 'new' poet, the author makes some attempt to cope with Whitman's universal enthusiasm and with the depths of his sympathy and thought. 'La poésie de Walt Whitman,' he says, 'proclama la première le panthéisme complet, sans atténuation, et avec toutes ses conséquences.' Sarrazin, too, affirms that Whitman is no artist: he is above art. A number of translations aim at illustrating his characteristics as a poet and the study ends with a warm appreciation of the man.

By this time some of the Symbolists had begun to work for a better understanding of Whitman. Two of them, Francis Vielé-Griffin and Stuart Merrill, happened to be Americans by birth and must have known of their compatriot from their earliest years. Both had come to France when quite young, and had ultimately settled in Paris. It was Vielé-Griffin who brought the *Leaves* to Jules Laforgue's attention with consequences to be noticed. The first of a series of more competent renderings were those by Laforgue which appeared in the tenth number of *La Vogue* in 1886, with the heading: 'M. Walt Whitman: Les Brins d'Herbe (Traduit de l'étonnant poète américain, Walt Whitman, J.L.)'.

After Laforgue's death Vielé-Griffin seems to have thought of translating extensively from Whitman and corresponded with him about an appropriate edition. But the project was not realized except for a number of pieces which he turned into French and published in *La Revue Indépendante* (1888), in *L'Ermitage* and *La Cravache* (1889), and in his own review, *Les Entretiens politiques et littéraires* (1892). Whitman's death in that year was the occasion for some obituary articles, to one of which we shall return. A few translations by Lawrence Jerrold were published in 1894. Then curiosity seems to have flagged until H. D. Davray proceeded with the work of translating from the *Leaves* in *La Plume* and *L'Ermitage* (1901-3).[1] Louis Fabulet followed with several renderings published during the next two years. In 1907 Elsie Masson wrote on Whitman, 'poète et ouvrier', in the *Mercure de France*, and in 1908 appeared Bazalgette's biography, *Walt Whitman, l'Homme et son Œuvre*, followed in the next year by his complete translation of the *Leaves*.

As for Stuart Merrill, he had always been an admirer of Whitman's work and was to defend him at a later period.[2] But although he frequently translated from the English poets, there is no record of his having attempted to turn any of the *Leaves* into French.

What is the significance of these essays and translations, published over a period of thirty years? Do they point to the intermittent attraction of a novelty, the naïve originality of the first Yankee poet? Or does the persistence with which certain French poets and critics have returned to the subject reveal the gradual discovery of a source of inspiration?

Nowhere has the question of the supposed influence of Whitman on the early Symbolists been so pertinently discussed as in an article which Téodor de Wyzewa published in *La Revue Bleue*

[1] That the interest was not dead in the interval is shown by the following point taken from *Marcel Schwob et son temps* by Pierre Champion, p. 78: 'Quant à l'américain Walt Whitman, Marcel Schwob le portait dans sa poche, traduisant chez Goncourt (*Journal* IX, p. 147, 21 July 1893), au courant de la lecture, *La Maison des Morts de la Cité*. Il lui doit non seulement une partie de son lyrisme, mais aussi des idées indiquées dans la préface de *Cœur double*: 'Mais la fin du siècle sera peut-être menée par la devise du poète Walt Whitman: *Soi-même et en masse*. La littérature célébrera les émotions violentes et actives.'

[2] See 'Pages d'un cahier de souvenirs, Verlaine et Walt Whitman', *Le Masque*, série II, nos. 9-10, 1912; 'Lettres pour répondre à Guillaume Apollinaire sur les funérailles de Walt Whitman', *Mercure de France*, CII, p. 89, 1913; 'La Question Walt Whitman', *Mercure de France*, 16 Nov. 1913.

at the time of the poet's death. In its insistence on resemblances and assumptions as well as in its ultimate denial of any contemporary influence, it summarized in 1892 conclusions which my own inquiries confirmed some twenty years later.

The writer of the article imagines future critics engaged upon the task of liquidating the literary achievement of nineteenth-century France. They will be astounded, he thinks, at what will appear to have been the enormous influence of Walt Whitman on the contemporary movement. They will be forced to recognize that of all the innovations attempted for twenty-five years in form, feeling and ideas, not one but is found indicated, realized, even exaggerated in the first volume of Whitman's poems. In the *Leaves* the writer finds not only the most radical naturalism, but free verse and subjective lyricism carried to their furthest extremes. Of the influence which another aspect of Whitman's poetry might have had on the younger poets, Wyzewa writes: 'On ne saurait leur proposer un plus enviable modèle de *compagnon de la vie nouvelle*, ou, comme on dit encore, de néo-chrétien.' When he is not 'singing himself', Whitman chants American democracy, including contemporary civilization, science and the latest progress in industry. Moreover, 'il s'attendrissait sans cesse'; he was emotional about railways, exhibitions, universal suffrage, the phonograph. Had he seen the Eiffel Tower, he would have been even more excited by it than is M. Henri Bérenger.[1] And as with Henri Bérenger and others, the sight of the modern world inspires him with an ethic of action and compassion. Even if it be maintained that the dominant trait of French literature for the last twenty-five years has been the search for novelty, in this too Whitman is acknowledged a forerunner.

[1] Author of a book of poems called *L'Âme moderne* (1892).

Then, reiterating that as far back as 1855 Whitman had practised all the innovations which had since been attempted in French literature, Téodor de Wyzewa denies the possibility of his influence. In the first place, very few contemporary writers knew Whitman, and those who did were not affected by him. In the second place, in spite of the apparent resemblance in sentiments, ideas and form, there was really nothing in common between his poetry and contemporary French poetry. Born in the nineteenth century, Whitman was none the less a primitive. The singularity of his poetry was not the result of reflection or of a desire to react from outworn traditions, but the spontaneous expression of his singular nature, itself the result of his origin, his temperament and the circumstances of his life.

Wyzewa's article is a *mise au point*, a judicious account of the situation of 'Whitman in France' up to the time of its appearance. The opposite point of view was put by Émile Blémont in 1904, when his pioneer essay reappeared in a book called *Beautés étrangères*. Blémont sums up in a postscript the position since 1872, as he now sees it. Referring to the free verse movement he speaks of the 'incontestable action' of Whitman, but without giving the slightest evidence. He was on safer ground in emphasizing Whitman's *priority* in the matter of literary innovation: 'Il réalisa d'avance le programme singulièrement élargi de nos écoles nouvelles.' Even here his affirmations remain vague. But the interest of both Blémont's postscript and Wyzewa's article is not what they affirm or deny, so much as what they imply. They show that long before the complete version appeared, not only were definite resemblances noticed between the ideas of Whitman and those of the Symbolists, but also that his work was held in certain quarters to have had considerable effect on the practice of their art.

II

The assumption that the Symbolists were in some way influenced by Whitman's example, though shared by Remy de Gourmont, does not seem capable of much definite proof. Most suggestions of the kind are made with reference to possible connections between the *vers libre* and the 'emancipated line' of *Leaves of Grass*. Otherwise, though there seem to be fairly abundant and authenticated signs of an influence exerted by Whitman's example on the *post*-Symbolist phase of French literature, it would, I think, be fruitless to look for much connection between his poems and those that were written in France from 1880 to the end of the century. The case is far from simple, however, and requires more to be done than to trace the steps of a growing interest in the *Leaves* and their author. Whitman, though he lived until 1892, could hardly be considered a contemporary of the Symbolists, the first edition of *Leaves of Grass* having appeared twenty years before *L'Après-midi d'un Faune*. Yet the fact that his work and theirs belong to the post-Romantic phase implies a common background of thought, sensibility and general technique. Actually in the speculations emanating from this background and in the formulation of a new poetic creed certain resemblances occur which seem worth attention. Here we have nothing comparable to the case of E. A. Poe—a demonstrable influence exerted by an admired model and admitted by its recipients. Instead we find two separate, and on the whole disparate, experimental developments ultimately converging on an enunciation of aims and principles which have a number of traits in common. Within the limits of the Symbolist movement, it might be said that the influence of Poe was the relatively easy acceptance of an approachable foreign master, while the receptivity to Whitman remained for long the tardy and partial recognition of a fascinating, but not easily assimilable, foreigner.

Let us, for the moment, abandon the quest for evidence of the effects of one author's work on the works of others, in favour of a comparison of some of the ideas on which these diverse experiments were based.

As a theorist Whitman subscribed to that conception of poetry as an indefinite art on which Poe had insisted and which Mallarmé and Verlaine were to re-formulate in turn. From the charge of obscurity Whitman defended himself in 1876 in terms which bear a curious resemblance to some of Mallarmé's. In the preface to an edition of *Leaves of Grass* and *Two Rivulets*, published that year, he wrote:

> In certain parts of these flights ... I have not been afraid of the charge of obscurity ... because human thought, poetry or melody, must leave dim escapes and outlets—must possess a certain fluid aerial character, akin to space itself, obscure to those of little or no imagination, but indispensable to the highest purposes. Poetic style, when address'd to the soul, is less definite form, outline, sculpture, and becomes vista, music, half-tints, and even less than half-tints. True, it may be architecture; but again it may be the forest wildwood, or the best effect thereof, at twilight, the waving oaks and cedars in the wind, and the impalpable odor.

Both the point of these remarks and the particular imagery employed remind one not only of Verlaine's emphasis on music and the nuance but of Mallarmé's dictum: 'Abolie, la prétention ... d'inclure au papier subtil du volume autre chose que par exemple l'horreur de la forêt, ou le tonnerre muet épars au feuillage: non le bois intrinsèque et dense des arbres.'[1]

It is remarkable how clearly Whitman saw the trend of coming

---

[1] *Relativement au Vers*, collected as *Crise de Vers* in *Divagations*.

changes. Recalling the best known of Mallarmé's pronouncements—'*Nommer* un objet c'est supprimer les trois quarts de la
jouissance du poème qui est faite du bonheur de deviner peu à
peu; le *suggérer*, voilà le rêve'[1]—we may note how radical the
main tenet of Symbolism was to the poetry of the latter half of
the nineteenth century by comparing Whitman's insistence on
indirectness and suggestion, even when he is emphasizing his
favourite types of realism. 'The poetry of the future', he wrote,

'aims at the free expression of emotion (which means far, far
more than appears at first) and to arouse and initiate, more than
to define or finish. Like all modern tendencies, it has direct or
indirect reference continually to the reader, to you or me, to the
central identity of everything, the mighty Ego. . . . Character, a
feature above style or polish . . . gives predominant stamp to
advancing poetry. Its born sister, music, already responds to the
same influences. . . .'[2]

And he quotes in translation that illuminating passage from
Sainte-Beuve which is a prototype of the Symbolist argument:

For us the greatest poet is he who in his works most stimulates
the reader's imagination and reflection, who excites him the most
himself to poetise. The greatest poet is not he who has done the
best; it is he who suggests the most; he not all of whose meaning
is at first obvious, and who leaves you much to desire, to explain,
to study, much to complete in your turn.'

The essence of this statement is summed up in the lines:

The words of the true poems give you more than poems,
They give you to form for yourself poems. . . .[3]

And again here:

The best poetic utterance, after all, can merely hint, or remind,

[1] Jules Huret, *Enquête sur l'Évolution Littéraire* (Paris, 1891), p. 60.
[2] *Complete Prose Works*, II, p. 216.
[3] *Leaves of Grass*, I, p. 205 (Camden Edition)

often very indirectly, or at distant removes. Aught of real perfection, or the solution of any deep problem, or any completed statement of the moral, the true, the beautiful, eludes the greatest, deftest poet—flies away like an always uncaught bird.[1]

Whitman constantly reminds the reader that his appeal is 'as much by indirections as by directions'. As for the *Leaves*—'The word I myself put primarily for the description of them as they stand at last is the word Suggestiveness.'[2]

> For it is not for what I have put into it that I have written this book,
> Nor is it by reading it you will acquire it . . .
> For all is useless without that which you may guess at many times and not hit, that which I hinted at.[3]

It is not of course implied that the Symbolists were familiar with these passages. They are cited to illustrate basic conceptions shared by Whitman, on the one hand, and by poets like Verlaine and Mallarmé on the other. On both sides of the Atlantic it seems to have been distinctly realized that poetry was akin to music and that the essential power of each was to suggest. But such coincidences are of too general a nature to furnish of themselves anything definite in support of a literary influence. The effect they seem to imply is not that of Whitman's own experiments and ruminations so much as the pervasive influence of E. A. Poe. The question arises whether the French poets, on the one hand, and Whitman, on the other, were not more or less simultaneously attracted by the example and theories of Poe. It is a question worth asking in the light of one of Whitman's admissions:

Toward the last I had among much else look'd over Edgar Poe's poems—of which I was not an admirer, tho' I always saw

---

[1] *Complete Prose Works*, III, p. 127. [2] *L. of G.* I, p. 141.
[3] *L. of G.* III, p. 58.

that beyond their limited range of melody (like perpetuate chimes of music bells, ringing from lower *b* flat up to *g*) they were melodious expressions, and perhaps never excell'd ones, of certain pronounc'd phases of human morbidity. (The Poetic area is very spacious—has room for all—has so many mansions!) But I was repaid in Poe's prose by the idea that (at any rate for our occasions, our day) there can be no such thing as a long poem. The same thought had been haunting my mind before, but Poe's argument, though short, work'd the sum and proved it to me.[1]

Nothing so far has been said about form, although, as will be seen later, most of the explicit assumptions were made with reference to that aspect of the influence. But before finishing with theory we may note that Whitman defended his own formal experiments in terms that fit almost perfectly into the programme of the *verslibristes*:

In my opinion [he wrote] the time has arrived to essentially break down the barriers of form between prose and poetry. I say the latter is henceforth to win and maintain its character regardless of rhyme, and the measurement-rules of iambic, spondee, dactyl, etc., and that ... the truest and greatest Poetry (while subtly and necessarily always rhythmic, and distinguishable easily enough) can never again, in the English language, be express'd in arbitrary and rhyming metre, any more than the greatest eloquence, or the truest power and passion. While admitting that the venerable and heavenly forms of chiming versification have in their time play'd great and fitting parts... it is, not withstanding, certain to me that the day of such conventional rhyme is ended.

This may bring to mind Verlaine's question about the validity of rhyme and his occasional abandonment of it in practice, or Mallarmé's tendency to efface in theory the difference between the rhythms of verse and of prose above the level of that used on

[1] *L. of G.* III, p. 56.

hoardings. But a far stronger comparison suggests itself when to the above remarks Whitman adds that the poetry of the future,

adapting itself to comprehend the size of the whole people, with the free play, emotions, pride, passions, experiences, that belong to them, body and soul—to the general globe, and all its relations in astronomy as the *savans* portray them to us—to the modern, the busy nineteenth century (as grandly poetic as any, only different) with steamships, railroads, factories, electric telegraphs, cylinder presses—to the thought of the solidarity of nations, the brotherhood and sisterhood of the entire earth—to the dignity and heroism of the practical labour of farms, factories, foundries, workshops, mines, or on shipboard, or on lakes and rivers—resumes that other medium of expression, more flexible, more eligible—soars to the freer, vast, diviner heaven of prose.[1]

Apart from prophesying the expansion of prose, this is the very programme and spirit of Verhaeren's attempt to conquer materialism and extend the powers of lyrical expression to the limits of the known cosmos. Yet even this obvious resemblance must not be pressed too far. The Belgian poet seems, for the greater part of his life, to have remained in ignorance of his forerunner's experiments, and we may recall that, before either, the aspiration to express modernity in a new medium had been briefly formulated by Baudelaire: 'C'est surtout de la fréquentation des villes énormes, c'est du croisement de leurs innombrables rapports que naît cet idéal obsédant.'[2]

III

Were it not for the evidence furnished in the first part of this chapter on the beginnings of a knowledge of Whitman in France and on the sporadic interest shown in his work and personality

[1] 'New Poetry', *Complete Prose Works*, II, pp. 272 ff.
[2] Preface to the *Petits Poèmes en Prose*.

during the Symbolist period, there would seem to be but one excuse, so far, for tabulating the points of analogy or comparison which have been discussed here—to *disprove* the suggestions of indebtedness made first and perhaps casually by certain French critics, yet reiterated frequently enough to provoke investigation. Even before we consider the question of form, we may admit that the differences between our terms of comparison are far more striking than the resemblances. These differences turn on relative degrees of sophistication and naturalness. The robust optimism of *Leaves of Grass* is, as their author perceived, in direct opposition to the morbid tendencies of Poe and, we may add, of Baudelaire, Mallarmé and the School. Most of the Symbolists were self-conscious artists drenched in traditions which cover even their naïveties with a patina of sophistication; much of their work conforms to a type the American would have abhorred— a *poésie d'élite*. Yet it is not altogether a paradox that a few of the most mannered of them—Laforgue, who was an original poet, and Stuart Merrill, who was mildly fastidious—should have been attracted to the 'étonnant poète américain'. The phrase itself indicates the nature of the curiosity and reminds us that a love of extreme individualism was characteristic of all the Symbolists. Actually, as we have seen, Merrill and Vielé-Griffin were drawn to Whitman by closer ties than curiosity. Of the nature of their interest it is now time to speak.

The successors of Verlaine and Mallarmé were far too dissimilar as personalities and as writers to constitute a group. But some of them—Vielé-Griffin, Laforgue, Stuart Merrill, Verhaeren, Francis Jammes and Paul Fort—had, despite individual distinctiveness, an attitude to life which differentiated them from their masters. They were positively and on the whole optimistically attracted to existence; they could be interested as poets in its concrete variety, in the forms and appearances of nature and in human reactions to them, in experience tragic or joyous, and in spiritual or scientific effort. Some of their interests were humanitarian. It is this generation certain writers have in mind when they call Symbolism a rich and vital synthesis; and it was, as we have seen, a few of its representatives who helped to introduce Whitman and to translate his poems. One critic, Philéas Lebesgue, was later to assert: 'Si le symbolisme avait compris dès le début sa propre grandeur il y a beau temps que le Barde de Manhattan aurait dû être revendiqué comme précurseur.'[1] And remembering that Whitman's 'sovereign theme' was

> . . . life immense in passion, pulse and power,
> Cheerful, for freest action form'd under laws divine,[2]

we may note that Vielé-Griffin claimed an equally comprehensive programme for Symbolism:

Ce qui caractérise le symbolisme, c'est la passion du mouvement au geste infini, de la Vie même, joyeuse ou triste, belle de toute la multiplicité de ses métamorphoses, passion agile et protéenne qui se confond avec les heures du jour et de la nuit, perpétuellement renouvelée, intarissable et diverse comme l'onde et le feu, riche du lyrisme éternel, prodigue comme la terre, puissante, profonde et voluptueuse comme le Mystère.[3]

It is hardly surprising that the year after this was written, its author was referred to as 'le petit-fils de Walt Whitman'.[4] Nor is that an isolated insinuation. Let us examine for a moment what such suggestions of direct poetic lineage amount to in the cases of Vielé-Griffin and his compatriot, Stuart Merrill.

---

[1] *La Phalange*, 15 June 1908.
[2] *L. of G.*, 'One's self I sing'.
[3] *Mercure de France*, October 1895.
[4] Maurice Le Blond, *Essai sur le naturisme.*

Like so many of the Symbolists, Vielé-Griffin began as a Parnassian. His Symbolist work dates from *Joies* (1889) and shows that fusion of influence, Wagnerian, Pre-Raphaelite, Swinburnian, which was active and prevalent at the time, as well as an equally characteristic adaptation of the spirit and manner of the *chanson populaire*. His later work is marked by a reversion to the legendary atmosphere of Christian and classical antiquity. This too represented a fairly general tendency. Such themes were the predominant literary sources from which Vielé-Griffin drew; and they are utterly non-Whitmanian. He was, however, by no means an exclusively literary poet. He could react to experience, to nature and especially to the spectacle of the Touraine countryside; and then his treatment differs considerably in spirit from that of his contemporaries, with the possible exception of Verhaeren in his later moods. The optimism which tempers his melancholy, his exhilarating sense of sunlight and of the wealth, mystery and beauty of life, struck notes that sounded fresh, positive and cheerful amid the dolorous undertones emitted by 'decadents and symbolists'—notes which seem to have reminded admirers of his alien origins. It was thus not unnatural for those who had heard of the 'astonishing American poet' whom he had helped to introduce, to predicate influence, when it might have been better to speak of consanguinity. Any more precise evidence I have never been able to deduce, either from his biography or from his works.

Whitmanian influence has also been suggested in connection with the humanitarian strain in Merrill's later work. His biographer, Miss M. L. Henry, discussed the point at some length.[1] The nearest resemblance seems to occur in Merrill's poem, *Le Vagabond* (*Les Quatre Saisons*, 1900), which she compares with

[1] M. L. Henry, *Stuart Merrill* (Paris, 1927). See especially p. 165.

Whitman's *Poem of the Road*. The theme is similar and may well have been suggested by Whitman. But in spirit and form the two pieces are very different. Whitman's is characteristic in a way Merrill's is not. The former writes out of his own experience; the latter, if not from a memory of Whitman, then from a mood or fancy which is not a permanent or recurrent part of his sensibility. None of Merrill's lines has the authentic Whitmanian ring. The contrast is all the more marked in that, having experimented in a kind of *vers libre* based on the tonic accent, Merrill here reverts to the alexandrine. Indeed most of the passages which Miss Henry compares seem to show more dissimilarity than resemblance. After this phrase from the *Poem of the Road*:

You shall be treated to the ironical smiles and mockings of those who remain behind you,

she quotes this from *Une Voix dans la foule*, which is merely *simpliste*:

> Même les tout petits enfants aux yeux si beaux
> Me suivront dans un bruit cliquetant de sabots
> Pour cracher sur mes pas et me jeter des pierres.

No attempt, however, is made to force a 'proof' out of any of these *rapprochements*. Miss Henry's conclusion is reasonable, if inconclusive. Referring to the democratic strain in *Les Quatre Saisons* and *Une Voix dans la foule* (1909), she says: 'Nous avons cru apercevoir dans Whitman—sinon la source même de ce sentiment—en tout cas une conception antérieure et très voisine. Actually, when we examine the humanitarian side of Merrill's work, it seems as if William Morris, whom he much admired, counted in practice for far more than Whitman. Merrill's humanitarian interests have an artistic reference similar to Morris's. His real attitude to both Whitman and Morris seems to be shown

in the phrase quoted by Miss Henry from a letter to the late
Professor Rudmose Brown: 'I sometimes dream of a poet who
would have been both Whitman and Morris, a Morris leaning
less toward things mediaeval, a Whitman with a greater charm of
expression. But I would give neither Whitman nor Morris, even
as they are, for that poet of my imagination.'[1]

IV

Except to a small but growing number of admirers, *Leaves of
Grass* was little known in France before 1908. Not only was a
reader's competence in English uncommon even among enthu-
siasts; the works themselves were difficult to find, the most
accessible edition being W. M. Rossetti's selection from which the
sex poems were excluded. Little by little curiosity was awakened.
'Whitmanists' were already in existence.

On nous interrogeait nous autres Whitmaniens [wrote M.
Valéry Larbaud in an interesting article published in 1909], on
nous demandait quel homme avait été ce Whitman, et on écoutait
attentivement nos traductions orales.—Vincent Muselli pourrait
témoigner que dès 1901-2, dans une chambre d'étudiant, rue de la
Sorbonne, quelques amis commémoraient, simplement mais avec
dignité, la naissance et la mort du Poète de la Démocratie. Quels
projets notre enthousiasme nous faisait faire alors! Je devais
parler sur 'Walt Whitman et la guerre de Sécession' dans une
sorte de cercle populaire, à Grenelle (j'ai encore mes notes). Nous
voulions proposer la vie de notre poète en exemple aux ouvriers!
De tout cela rien ne sortit et l'article que je destinais à *La Plume*
(et que son directeur a longtemps attendu) fut retardé de mois en
mois par des circonstances indépendantes de ma volonté, jusqu'à
la disparition de *La Plume*, et ne fut jamais achevé. Je crois bien
que plusieurs articles et des traductions de nombreuses pièces des

[1] *Op. cit.* p. 228.

Feuilles d'herbe furent ainsi préparés, et ne virent jamais le jour, pour des motifs restés inexpliqués, ou plutôt par une sorte de fatalité singulière.[1]

This article reveals clearly enough the nature of the interest that flourished and fluctuated in Paris before the War. The year before it appeared, a book on *Walt Whitman, l'Homme et son Œuvre*, had been produced by the *Mercure de France*. The first biography of the poet to appear in French, it was the work of Léon Bazalgette, one of the most fervent of all devotees of Whitman. In 1909 came his complete version of *Leaves of Grass*, which, before that date, had been translated entirely only into Italian. The definite phase of the influence begins with the appearance of these two works. But Bazalgette's translations failed to satisfy the more fastidious of his compatriots who could read Whitman in the original. In 1918 the *Nouvelle Revue Française* brought out a selection from the poems and prose works, translated by some half-dozen men of letters, and including the original renderings by Laforgue and Vielé-Griffin. This is undoubtedly the best literary monument raised so far to Whitman's memory in France.

Expanding curiosity had already found one of its liveliest centres in 'L'Abbaye', a group of writers and artists established at Créteil in 1906. A fairly recent account of this movement contains an estimate of the effect Whitman had upon its members.[2] M. Jules Romains, who was in close touch with the movement, has always denied any personal debt to the American poet. But

---

[1] *La Phalange*, 20 April 1909. M. Valéry Larbaud's *Barnabooth* (1913) shows, in its poetical section, some obvious adaptations of Whitman's mannerisms.

[2] M. L. Bidal, *Les Écrivains de l'Abbaye*, Boivin, pp. 48-66. Cf. Georges Duhamel, 'Le Temps de la Recherche (III)', *Mercure de France*, 1 March 1947, p. 499.

M. Charles Vildrac was far from asserting an equal independence. 'Nul moment de littérature', he wrote as late as 1913, 'ne pouvait être plus favorable que celui-ci à notre découverte de Whitman. . . . L'œuvre du barde de Manhattan s'implante chez nous comme un grand arbre du nouveau monde.'[1]

When, in the same year, M. Georges Duhamel, reviewing a new edition of Mallarmé's *Poésies*, could conduct a fairly sustained, if not conclusive, comparison between Mallarmé and Whitman—introducing Rimbaud to finish off the *chronique*[2]— it scarcely seems too much to say that the American poet had by then been accepted, in company with the leading Symbolists, as one of the masters of a new generation.

---

[1] *Les Feuilles de Mai*, no. 3, April-June 1913.
[2] *Mercure de France*, 1 April 1913: *Rubrique, Les Poèmes.*

PART TWO

THE EMERGENCE OF THE
VERS LIBRE

J'apporte en effet des nouvelles les plus
surprenantes. Même cas ne se vit encore.
—On a touché au vers.

MALLARMÉ
La Musique et les Lettres 1894

NOTE

The *vers libre* or modern French free verse has been a topic of ceaseless discussion, a veritable apple of discord, since it ripened on one of the ramifying branches of French versification during the middle eighties of last century. What has been written on the subject is, almost all of it, tendentious. No comprehensive treatment has been given either to the history or to what may be called the 'mystery' of the phenomenon. Work like Robert de Souza's shows a serious, if biased, attempt to tackle the problem along technical lines; whereas modern manuals of French versification have tended to avoid recent variations or vagaries more or less completely. For Maurice Grammont, author of the best known of these, the only *vers libre* worth attention was that variety of the traditional versification characteristic of the fables of La Fontaine. In an essay published in Paris in 1923 on *Les Techniques Modernes du Vers Français*, M. Jean Hytier, with a glance at 'L'Anarchie verslibriste', turned to expound the technique proposed and practised by M. Jules Romains and the group of L'Abbaye who were in conscientious reaction from disorder.

At the head of his list of references M. Hytier placed the *Essai sur l'Histoire du Vers français* by Professor Hugo P. Thieme of Michigan University.[1] The importance of this work is bibliographical. It covers the development of the theory of French verse-writing from the Middle Ages to the Symbolist period. Hardly a line of French poetry is quoted and no special light is thrown on the nature of recent developments. But Professor Thieme's work is useful and premonitory. It contains some wise

[1] Paris, 1916.

91

reservations—if not about the new form itself—at least with reference to the problem it presents.

The essence of that problem lies in the nature of French rhythm. Without a surer knowledge of what Robert de Souza called 'Du Rhythme en Français' (I refer to the subject, not the work itself) we are hardly likely to advance very far. Professor Thieme is aware of this: 'La nature exacte du rythme dans la poésie française reste encore à définir.' Gustave Lanson, who wrote a preface for his work, complimented the author on having admitted that, after all, 'les Français eux-mêmes ont seuls le sens intime et subtil de leur propre vers et de son rythme'. With this warning and the forbearance it implies I am in sympathy. Without an exceptional degree of intimacy with a language and its poetry, regarded both intuitively and technically, it would be folly to make pronouncements on the essentials of rhythm as opposed to the externals of prosody and scansion. This seems especially true in the case of a language which is not one's own. Yet such folly has been indulged in by German and (less frequently) British investigators, who have attempted to solve the mystery by assimilating the rhythm of French poetry to that of their native poetry and who appear to deserve the reproof Professor Thieme administers. No such ambition has inspired the chapters that follow. What I have attempted here is to sketch, with the help of commentators, the emergence of a mode and of a theory from the sequence of experiments and the conflict of ideas attendant upon the movement of liberation from traditional moulds and rules, which were felt increasingly to be restrictive and obstructive during the middle decades of the nineteenth century.[1]

[1] A few more recent works on modern French poetic rhythm are mentioned in the Bibliographies.

CHAPTER V

FROM POETIC PROSE TO THE PROSE-POEM

I

'A RIOT of versification: that, you know,' said Heredia to Jules Huret, 'was all the Symbolist movement was at bottom —*a revolution in form.*'[1] This was but one of several assertions of the kind, ranging from Remy de Gourmont's identification of the effort with a 'brisement du vers' to Gustave Kahn's positive contention that the crown of the movement was the production of the *vers libre*. Yet to lay exclusive stress on the formal aspect would be to forget that Symbolism stood for a method—it has often been said, for a *mystique*—more even than for a form, and that those who cultivated the method were not invariably those who did most for the freeing of French verse. Acknowledged leaders like Mallarmé and Verlaine ignored the *vers libre* in their own practice, Verlaine scornfully, Mallarmé professing a fervent interest in 'this adventure'. Mallarmé indeed was to make one experiment in free rhythms of a complex and audacious character. By the time it appeared, however, the *vers libre* had become almost an accepted mode; and the master's '*Coup de dés*' throws less light on the origins of free verse than on the technical pre-occupations of the period as reflected and amplified in its subtlest mind. Most of his contemporaries, like the poets in his *Phénomène futur*, were 'hantés du Rythme'. What was originally meant by the term '*vers libre*' we shall attempt to inquire later. It would be futile to begin with definitions. First because of the difficulty

[1] Jules Huret, *op. cit.*, p. 303.

93

of defining a phenomenon, the 'spontaneous' name for which seems to present a contradiction in terms—'verse' implying restriction—a contradiction, verbal perhaps, but suggestive of a desire for new adjustments between the rhythmical impulse and formal demands. And again because the name covers a variety of experimental types. A few basic principles were observed by all the innovators. But as divergencies in the use of a 'free' form may and did increase very rapidly, the question arises: Whose *vers libre* is to be defined? That too we shall have to postpone until we have considered some of the developments that led up to the innovation itself.

Theoretically what the *verslibristes* were seeking was an infinitely variable medium compatible with their ideal of unrestricted freedom in opposition to the limitations and restraints of metre. 'La liberté la plus grande: qu'importe le nombre du vers, si le rythme est beau?'[1] The use of the alexandrine was not categorically excluded. But the appearance of the *vers libre* marks a stage which was conceived by many of its exponents as a complete breakaway from the traditional versification. It was to be not just another variation but a new thing and, like all literary and artistic innovations, it owes its existence primarily to a change of sensibility. 'Le rythme fixe', it was said, 'ne peut plus exprimer notre sensibilité. Il nous faut aujourd'hui des vers qui lui soient adéquats.' Classics and Romantics had written masterpieces, the former using a 'bad', the latter an 'excellent', instrument. 'Mais', said Kahn, 'si l'oreille des romantiques différait de celle des classiques, la nôtre a d'autres besoins que les leurs.' The contemporary ear, he insisted, was attuned to music, and this led to a perception of poetic form at once more fluid and more precise.

Mallarmé found literature in his time undergoing 'une exquise

---

[1] Henri de Régnier to Jules Huret, *op. cit.* p. 94.

crise fondamentale'. A complete lack of common understanding separated the Parnassians, perpetually 'vilipendés', from the Symbolists, invariably dismissed as 'fumistes'. 'Que d'animosités, grands dieux!' exclaimed the Belgian onlooker, Edmond Picard. In their revolt against the impersonal art of their immediate predecessors, the innovators of the 'eighties and the 'nineties were intent upon carrying the poetry of self-conscious subjectivism to unprecedented extremes. A couple of decades of Parnassian rigour had provoked reactions in favour of a new lyrical medium, capable ideally of the utmost modulation and adaptable to the most intimate perceptions, the subtlest and most bizarre moods of the individual poet. Produced in an atmosphere of heated discussion and accompanied in its development by a host of theories, the *vers libre* was in the first instance, not the product of a theory, but an innovation corresponding to an acutely felt need. That it was a novelty which encouraged absurd extravagances is true. But the extravagances were aggravated by obtuse resistances. Compare these two statements:

Dois-je dire que ni Corneille ni Molière ni la plupart des écrivains en vers de notre siècle ne furent vraiment des Poètes? Une convention les forçait à déformer leurs pensées pour les soumettre à un rythme fixe et inintelligent, à des rimes superflues.[1]

Is that really more fatuous than the Parnassian assurance reflected in Sully Prudhomme's phrase: ' . . . la technique des vers est achevée'?

II

Huret, in one of his best interviews, records an anecdote told with gusto by Heredia, of a young poet who, when his elder protested against a line of seventeen syllables, knocked off two

[1] T. de Wyzewa, 'L'Art Wagnérien: Littérature', *Revue Wagnérienne*, VI, 1886.

and said: 'There won't be more than fifteen now, that's all.' For us the story has a different sense from that intended by the narrator. Heredia and his contemporaries appear not to have suspected that their juniors were trying to create a new versification in which syllables do not count anyhow. The nearest offended dignity could come to comprehension was to call the result 'prose rythmée', and that suggests a connection.

Questioned on the origins of *verslibrisme*, most of its devotees would point to the emancipated versification of Verlaine as the prior stage from which emerged modern French free verse in general and their own experiments in particular. Some, however, of its most ardent exponents denied Verlaine so influential a place among their predecessors. Recalling his vehement intolerance of the incipient *verslibrisme* of his day, they turned to look for more authentic sources in the development of poetic prose during the later nineteenth century or in the influence of foreign models. Such views, though partial and limited, are not unsound so far as they go. But they failed to satisfy an investigator like Robert de Souza, who attempted a scientific inquiry into the origins and essentials of French rhythm and accentuation, and who regarded such contributions as Verlaine's versification and modern poetic prose as more or less incidental in an evolution proceeding from the liberty of medieval metres and rhythms. This, however, is a long-distance view. As we intend to deal with nineteenth-century developments only, we shall have to confine ourselves to the more immediate background and issues of the movement.

Of the two precursory forms Verlaine's verse was probably—despite Verlaine's attitude—the more influential. But earlier developments, operating outside the sphere of *metrical* emancipation, had results which were by no means unimportant. Any account of the beginnings of free verse, however cursory, would be incomplete without some reference to the contribution made by the shaping of prose as medium for a context of poetical quality. This had been happening since Fénelon. Admirers of *Télémaque* gave his most popular work the title of 'poème en prose', and the genre had many devotees.[1] Subsequent developments were by no means confined to the eighteenth-century prose epic; long before the middle of the last century they had produced a type of prose, fairly definite in cadence and purpose, conceived almost as an equivalent, if not as a rival, of lyrical form.

The distance between poetical prose and the prose-poem is one of degree rather than of kind and was not originally stressed. Parts of the prose works of the great Romantics show the elements of rhythm, imagination and feeling fused in paragraphs of high intensity or concentration. A chapter in *Les Misérables* called 'L'Homme à la mer' is in this sense a prose-poem. For his *Paroles d'un Croyant* Lamennais chose a biblical style and manner and a form resembling that of the Psalms. Gradually, in contradistinction to its earlier vague acceptation, the term came to imply a detached, scrupulously wrought fragment, produced with strict attention to form and effect. The prototype in the nineteenth century is a small volume of prose cameos called *Gaspard de la Nuit* by Aloïsius (Louis) Bertrand. Brought out posthumously in 1842 with an introduction by Sainte-Beuve, they were described by him as 'petites ballades en prose, dont le couplet ou le verset exact simulait assez bien la cadence d'un rythme'. And he added: 'On en a eu l'application, depuis, dans le livre traduit des *Pèlerins polonais* et dans les *Paroles d'un Croyant*.'

During the last decade of his life, Charles Baudelaire attempted

[1] See Vista Clayton, *The Prose-Poem in French Literature of the Eighteenth Century* (New York).

to apply Bertrand's method in his *Petits Poèmes en Prose*.[1] Hardly had he begun, when he perceived that he was doing something 'singularly different', as he wrote to Arsène Houssaye. The following points from his letter, which now serves as preface to the collected edition, show the nature of this divergence:

> ... en feuilletant, pour la vingtième fois au moins, le fameux *Gaspard de la Nuit* d'Aloysius Bertrand ... l'idée m'est venue de tenter quelque chose d'analogue et d'appliquer à la description de la vie moderne, ou plutôt d'*une* vie moderne et plus abstraite, le procédé qu'il avait appliqué à la peinture de la vie ancienne, si étrangement pittoresque.
>
> Quel est celui de nous qui n'a pas, dans ses jours d'ambition, rêvé le miracle d'une prose poétique, musicale sans rythme et sans rime, assez souple et assez heurtée pour s'adapter aux mouvements lyriques de l'âme, aux ondulations de la rêverie, aux soubresauts de la conscience?
>
> C'est surtout de la fréquentation des villes énormes, c'est du croisement de leurs innombrables rapports que naît cet idéal obsédant ...

It could hardly be conceded that all the pieces in this collection conform to the purest type of prose poetry, or even that the ideal indicated in the letter to Houssaye is realized in most of them. Many are anecdotes, some approximate to short stories. In a fair number, however, the poetical intention is achieved, in a few brilliantly. *L'Étranger*, which opens the series, is one of the most perfect of Baudelaire's shorter poems:

—Qui aimes-tu le mieux, homme énigmatique, dis? ton père, ta mère, ta sœur ou ton frère?
—Je n'ai ni père, ni mère, ni sœur, ni frère.
—Tes amis?

[1] The first group to be published appeared in a review called *Le Présent* in 1857. The series was collected posthumously in 1869.

—Vous vous servez là d'une parole dont le sens m'est resté jusqu'à ce jour inconnu.

—Ta patrie?

—J'ignore sous quelle latitude elle est située.

—La beauté?

—Je l'aimerais volontiers, déesse et immortelle.

—L'or?

—Je le hais comme vous haïssez Dieu.

—Eh! qu'aimes-tu donc, extraordinaire étranger?

—J'aime les nuages . . . les nuages qui passent . . . là-bas . . . là-bas . . . les merveilleux nuages!

M. Ernest Raynaud has pointed out that while Baudelaire was not the first Frenchman to write prose-poems, he was the first to 'present the formula'.[1] Neither his formula nor his achievement was in the line of Bertrand's work. *Gaspard de la Nuit* bears the subtitle, *Fantaisies à la manière de Rembrandt et de Callot.* It is a specimen of Romantic writing, deliberately pictorial in design, etched sepias or genre paintings realized statically in words. Baudelaire's ambition was to draw upon the resources of music and movement. He aimed at a poetic prose which should be 'musical'; and if an ancestry had to be found for this type, I should suggest that one of its sources might be traced to the 'impassioned prose' of De Quincey's *Confessions of an Opium Eater,* of which Baudelaire had given an adaptation before the greater number of his own prose-poems could have been written. What the letter to Houssaye implies is that *Gaspard de la Nuit* was the incentive, not the model, for the *petits poèmes.* But the important point is that Baudelaire's type, not Bertrand's, became the standard for the future. In the opinion of admirers and imitators both model and

---

[1] In his preface to the Garnier edition of the *Petits Poèmes en Prose* (Paris, 1928). But see the important 'Introduction aux Petits Poèmes en Prose de Baudelaire' by M. Georges Blin, *Fontaine,* 48-49 (Feb. 1946).

formula were most perfectly realized in the piece called *Les Bien-faits de la Lune*—a complete unit which resists quotation unless it be given whole; but for that there is no space here.

After Baudelaire the number increases of those who experiment in forms intermediate between verse and prose. One of the most eccentric was Charles Cros, whose *Coffret de Santal* (1873) contains a non-metrical, humorous piece, 'Hareng Saur', which delighted Verlaine and his contemporaries. Another remarkable 'artisan du rythme' belonging to the transitional period was Villiers de l'Isle-Adam. *Axël*, though not written in verse, is a supremely poetical drama. For his few poems, full of Symbolist subtlety and grace, Villiers used the recognized metres—except, one may note, in the two small songs which occur at the end of *Axël*, Ukko's and the 'Chanson des Bûcherons'. These in their diminutive compass seem authentic examples of early *vers libres*, the last part of the drama having appeared in *La Jeune France* for 1 June 1886. Mallarmé's contribution is later but far more important.

III

The poetry of Mallarmé is written almost entirely in the 'liberated' form of the traditional versification. In 1887, when he acknowledged a volume of René Ghil's poems, he evidently believed in the autonomy of the single verse, and found Ghil's not sufficiently 'un joyau significatif à manier pour le regard et faisant poids dans la main'.[1] This strikes a distinctly Parnassian note. Unlike Verlaine, however, Mallarmé was not unfavourably disposed to free verse. In theorizing he tended to efface the accepted external distinctions. 'Verse', he told Jules Huret,

is everywhere in language where there is rhythm, except in posters

[1] René Ghil, *Les Dates et les Œuvres*, p. 92.

and the advertisement page of newspapers. There are verses in what is called prose, sometimes admirable ones and in all manner of rhythms. But in truth there is no prose: there is the alphabet and then verses more or less concise or diffuse. Wherever there is effort towards style, there is versification.

Mallarmé's use of poetic prose was first exemplified in his prose-poems, some of which, like *Pauvre Enfant Pâle* and *La Pipe*, had appeared as early as 1865, and in his translations from the poems of E. A. Poe, which came out at intervals in the course of 1872.[1] Six years later he produced a reprint of Beckford's *Vathek* with a prefatory essay in 'symphonic prose' and in 1897 came his *Divagations*, which open with thirteen pieces in rhythmical prose called *Anecdotes ou poèmes*.[2] M. Jean Royère, writing in 1912, considered this new prose, initiated by Mallarmé and developed by his successors, to be the most fruitful reform effected in French poetry by the Symbolists. 'Je crois très sincèrement', he said, 'que là est l'avenir de notre poésie.'[3]

Towards the end of his life Mallarmé had been meditating new possibilities. Opinions vary as to whether his supreme experiment, the mysteries of which continue to enthral and defeat commentators, should be considered, formally, as an example of poetic prose or of the freest of free verse. The proselytizing Kahn claimed the result as the master's unique contribution to the new form, made at his own instigation. Albert Thibaudet, in his book on Paul Valéry, affirmed that neither Valéry nor Mallarmé had been touched by the *vers libre* or had touched the *vers libre*. But Mallarmé himself had, as we shall see, a compromise in mind. The piece in question appeared in 1897 in an international review

[1] In *La Renaissance artistique et littéraire*. See E. Noulet, *L'Œuvre poétique de Mallarmé* (Paris, 1940), p. 524.
[2] They had appeared separately in the interval.
[3] See Emile Henriot, *A quoi rêvent les jeunes gens*, p. 21.

called *Cosmopolis*,[1] and had for title its first phrase: *Un coup de dés jamais n'abolira le Hasard*. In a preface of a few hundred words the author offers an explanation of the extraordinary appearance of his poem.[2] His note begins with apologies first to the 'skilful' reader for telling him little beyond what his own penetration would perceive, then to the 'ingenuous' reader who may be distracted from keeping his eyes on the sequence from the first words to the last. For the historian the prefatory note is full of interest and illuminates Mallarmé's attitude not only to his own work but to the problems of form at his time and at ours. As little has been written about this experiment in our country, let us attempt not a translation but what may be called a summary paraphrase of the note.

Mallarmé claims no novelty except for the way the piece is spaced. What strikes the eye first and assumes importance are the blanks. In ordinary versification the white portions of the page run alongside the print; they constitute a 'silence' round the poem and occupy about a third of the surface. The author of *Un coup de dés* does not transgress this measure; he merely disperses it: 'Le papier intervient chaque fois qu'une image, d'elle-même, cesse ou rentre.' As there is no question here of the regular beat of verse but of what he calls 'prismatic subdivisions of the Idea', the moment of their appearance and disappearance in a precise spiritual context, allowance must be made for their variability relative to the leading theme with as much verisimilitude as possible. The literary advantage of this way of separating

---

[1] No. 17, March 1897. The poem was published separately by the N.R.F. in 1914.

[2] It was accompanied by an editorial note which emphasized the musical preoccupations underlying the innovation. Several different types were used to differentiate the components of the poem. Punctuation was omitted.

the word groups or the words themselves from one another is that it accelerates or slows down the movement, scanning it, intimating it in accordance with a simultaneous view of the Page —the latter being taken as the unit, like the Verse or perfect line in the older prosody.

The device is to begin with a dominant phrase stated from the title and continued with subsidiary or ephemeral developments. Everything proceeds by condensation and hypothesis; narration is avoided. Add that this method results, when read aloud, in giving the effect of a musical score. The difference of the characters in which the work is printed marks the importance, for oral transmission, of the preponderant and secondary motifs and of subsidiary developments; and the position, high, low or middle of the page, indicates the rise or fall of intonation.

Mallarmé then refers to the limits imposed by publication. Certain 'very bold directions' remain in an elementary state in a work that lacks precedents, not because he thinks this the moment for timid experiments, but because it would not become him— apart from a special pagination or a volume of his own—to act in a fashion too contrary to usage, even in a Periodical which shows itself gracious and inviting to liberties. In any case he will have indicated a 'state' of his own Poem not at variance in all points with the tradition; he will have carried his experiment far enough to open people's eyes without offending them. Today— and without predicting what the future has in store for this kind of experiment, whether nothing at all or almost a new art—he is ready to acknowledge that his attempt participates in pursuits special or dear to his time—the *vers libre* and the poem in prose. Their reunion is accomplished under an extraneous influence, that of Music heard in the concert room. Finding that music employs many of the means belonging to Literature, he reclaims them ('je les reprends'). The new genre—may it become one like the symphony beside solo-singing—leaves intact the old verse-form, for which he professes a cult and to which he attributes the empire of passion and reverie; whereas it is now a case of treating for preference (as is being done in what follows) certain subjects of pure or complex imagination or of the intellect, which there is no reason to exclude from Poetry—the unique source.

To comment on a piece of Mallarmé's writing is to run as many risks as in attempting to paraphrase or translate. Apart from what he says, his use of language is so personal that its shades and subtleties evade the most attentive interpreter. Certain points in the note seem, however, to stand out clearly and prompt an observation or two.

It may be with a touch of that delicate irony for which he was famous that Mallarmé refers to the ingenuous reader. What is probably implied by the contrast with the skilful reader is the possibility of a spontaneous and intuitive perception even of work as complex and meditated as his own. The fact that to appreciate the rhythm of his poem requires 'une vision simultanée de la Page' reinforces this impression. His novel mode of presentation is intended to strike the eye; and he evidently thinks that what will first attract attention are the 'blancs'. The French word is an instance of 'ambiguity', being used here in two senses—for white spaces and for musical rests. But to substitute the word 'rests' in our paraphrase would cut more than half the meaning out of the text.

To the word 'Idée' also we must give a wide connotation. A poem by Mallarmé is not just an idea 'clothed' in poetic form. We may recall his answer when Degas complained that if he could not finish a certain sonnet, it was not through lack of ideas. 'You don't write poetry with ideas', said Mallarmé, 'but with words.' His use of the word 'idée' in the note suggests 'theme'. If, however, we think of the impulse as creating a spontaneous rhythm of its own instead of adopting the stereotyped rhythm of metre, we begin to see the contrast which Mallarmé (and the *verslibristes* of his time) had in mind, that between, on the one hand, a form closely adapted to the variability of the movement which it aims at reproducing with *verisimilitude*, and, on the other, the traditional fixed form with its regular sonorities.

The mode of *Un coup de dés* is not identified by its author with either the *vers libre* or the prose-poem exclusively. He claims to unite both in a new form which appropriates still more from orchestration and approximates to the symphony. The old versification he proposes to reserve for special purposes. This implies at least a partial break with the tradition. Mallarmé, it is interesting to find, suggests that his new 'prosody' should be reserved for purely imaginative or intellectual subjects. It has so often been implied that he aimed at a 'pure poetry' in which sound counts for everything, sense for nothing, that the diversity of his ideal should be underlined as well as the hint of a role for the intellect. The whole argument is found condensed in this paragraph from *Crise de vers* (*Divagations*), which is worth meditating:

Certainement, je ne m'assieds jamais aux gradins des concerts, sans percevoir parmi l'obscure sublimité telle ébauche de quelqu'un des poèmes immanents à l'humanité ou leur originel état, d'autant plus compréhensible que tu et que pour en déterminer la vaste ligne le compositeur éprouva cette facilité de suspendre jusqu'à la tentation de s'expliquer. Je me figure par un indéracinable sans doute préjugé d'écrivain, que rien ne demeurera sans être proféré; que nous en sommes là, précisément, à rechercher, devant une brisure des grands rythmes littéraires (il en a été question plus haut) et leur éparpillement en frissons articulés proches de l'instrumentation, un art d'achever la transposition, au Livre, de la symphonie ou uniment de reprendre notre bien: car, ce n'est pas de sonorités élémentaires par les cuivres, les cordes, les bois, indéniablement mais de l'intellectuelle parole à son apogée que doit avec plénitude et évidence, résulter, en tant que l'ensemble des rapports existant dans tout, la Musique.

It may seem a digression to conclude by evoking the name of E. A. Poe. But Mallarmé admired him without restraint and was so intimately acquainted with his work and ideas[1] that it is perhaps not far-fetched to suggest that the final phrase of his note, 'Poésie—unique source', might be read in the light of Poe's insistence, in the most famous of his essays, on Poetic Sentiment as the basis of all the arts.

From the chronological standpoint Arthur Rimbaud ought to have been mentioned earlier, *Les Illuminations* having appeared first in 1886 in *La Vogue*. The collection contains a number of poems in *vers libérés* with two small pieces in *vers libres*, to which we shall return. The greater part are fragments of poetic prose. Special circumstances connected with Rimbaud's life and reputation prejudiced many minds against his aggressive genius and uningratiating manners, and his disappearance seemed to them, one suspects, a total and beneficent eclipse. Official criticism remained obtuse. As late as 1902 Catulle Mendès in his *Rapport sur le mouvement poétique français* dismissed Rimbaud as a 'Pétrus Borel naturaliste'. So that work which contains the germ and model of many recent audacities and which is now regarded as the most original literary phenomenon of the late nineteenth century was able to exert little or no direct influence on the developments we have so far considered.

[1] One need only turn to the index of Mondor's *Vie de Mallarmé* for evidence.

Not that Rimbaud is negligible; indeed he was exceptional in this as in other matters. Contrasting his achievement with that of the great artisans of the genre who preceded him, Dr Enid Starkie writes: 'With Rimbaud the prose poem is generally stripped of all its anecdotic narrative and even descriptive content and it becomes highly concentrated and short.'[1] The first of the three pieces called *Veillées* is given as typical of his method:

C'est le repos éclairé, ni fièvre, ni langueur, sur le lit ou sur le pré.
C'est l'ami ni ardent ni faible. L'ami.
C'est l'aimée ni tourmentante ni tourmentée. L'aimée.
L'air et le monde point cherchés. La vie.
—Était-ce donc ceci?
—Et le rêve fraîchit.

Dr Starkie also reveals another precedent. Pointing out how many of the *Illuminations* are succinct, almost detachable phrases, she relates these to the form adopted for the translation of Chinese poems, frequently made towards the close of the Second Empire, especially in Parnassian circles. The most attractive example is *Le Livre de Jade* by Judith, daughter of Théophile Gautier, which appeared 1867. In 1872 she was publishing prose poems of her own in *La Renaissance artistique et littéraire*, to which review during the same half-year Mallarmé was sending his first translations of Poe and in which Rimbaud's poem, *Les Corbeaux*, appeared on 14 September 1872.

For us, however, there appears to be an earlier and more germane model with which the dominant form and type of *Les Illuminations* may be associated and which Rimbaud's adolescent curiosity could hardly have missed. In the pockets of Gérard de Nerval after his suicide was found the manuscript of a

---

[1] Enid Starkie, *Arthur Rimbaud* (1947), p. 225.

work which might suggest comparison with the *Confessions* of De Quincey but for the superior finesse, the unearthly pathos and magic of what must be the most marvellous specimen of dream literature in French. This was *Aurélia ou le Rêve et la Vie*, which appeared in print soon after the author's death in 1855. To the unfinished manuscript were appended a number of letters in the same strain, and finally under the title of *Mémorables* (adopted from Swedenborg) came some further 'impressions de plusieurs rêves' in fragmentary form. Earlier in these studies (p. 10), I referred to *Aurélia* as the record of an *askesis* through the occult. Dr Starkie has shown that Rimbaud passed through a similar experience. Whether there is a connection here or not, an unmistakable resemblance occurs between parts and aspects of these two works. Compare, for instance, *Après le Déluge*, the first poem in *Les Illuminations*, with this the first of Gérard's *Mémorables*. No verbal parallels will be found; but in each case the pristine spontaneity or post-diluvian freshness is matched by the variable, interrupted rhythms of detachable paragraphs of lyrical prose:

Sur un pic élancé de l'Auvergne a retenti la chanson des pâtres. *Pauvre Marie*! *Reine des cieux*! c'est à toi qu'ils s'adressent pieusement. Cette mélodie rustique a frappé l'oreille des corybantes. Ils sortent, en chantant à leur tour, des grottes secrètes où l'amour leur fit des abris.—Hosannah! paix à la terre et gloire aux cieux!

Sur les montagnes de l'Himalaya une petite fleur est née.—Ne m'oubliez pas.—Le regard chatoyant d'une étoile s'est fixé un instant sur elle, et une réponse s'est fait entendre dans un doux langage étranger.—*Myosotis*!

Une perle d'argent brillait dans le sable; une perle d'or étincelait au ciel. . . Le monde était créé. Chastes amours, divins soupirs! enflammez la sainte montagne. . . car vous avez des frères dans les vallées, et des sœurs timides qui se dérobent au sein des bois! . . .

So brilliant a series of experiments, to which the most talented writers of the period contributed, was bound to affect the art of poetry and the craft of versification and, in particular, to promote the rapid devolution of rhythm. To trace the consequences of this movement would be beyond the scope of our survey. Let us conclude this brief treatment of an aspect by borrowing a phrase from one of the most active and observant, if not one of the most impressive, of Symbolist poets: 'Le poème en prose était la tentative de libérer la poésie en prenant la prose pour point de départ; le vers libre et le verset représentent la même tentative en partant du vers . . . .'[1]

---

[1] Édouard Dujardin, *Mallarmé*, p. 188.

CHAPTER VI

THE *VERS LIBÉRÉ*

BETWEEN 1870 and 1887 the fetters of Parnassian versification
were being loosened by men, some of whom represent a new
era in French poetry—Paul Verlaine, Stéphane Mallarmé,
Arthur Rimbaud, and it is customary to add, for his *bruyant* but
temporary adherence, Jean Moréas. In their hands the stiff,
marmoreal verse established by the preceding school underwent
a series of dislocations and transformations, which modified its
contours and structure and remodelled it in accordance with an
ideal more nearly akin to music than to the plastic and pictorial
arts. Meanwhile the strict Parnassians resisted the desecration of
their cherished medium with protests of indignation and dismay.

As with all innovations, many of the technical changes
introduced by the 'decadents', as they were called, had been fore-
shadowed in the works or theories of their predecessors. In his
Petit Traité de Poésie française (1872), Théodore de Banville
expressed regret that Hugo, 'cet Hercule victorieux aux mains
sanglantes', had not carried to its logical conclusion the revolution in the art of verse which he inaugurated. French verse, he
admitted, no longer crawls in the mire. But he would have liked
to see it rise so high in the air that its wings escaped all barriers
and obstacles:

J'aurais voulu que le poète, délivré de toutes les conventions
empiriques, n'eût d'autre maître que son oreille délicate, subtilisée
par les plus douces caresses de la musique. En un mot, j'aurais

voulu substituer la Science, l'Inspiration, la Vie toujours renou-velée et variée à une Loi mécanique et immobile.

Banville insisted with the ardour of a Symbolist on the musi-cality of verse. In the case of certain technicalities—the caesura, for instance—he demanded the greatest possible liberty. But the excessive importance he attached to rhyme and the traditional rhythms prevents us from regarding him as a precursor of *vers-librisme*. An expert Parnassian, anchored to a narrow art which he manipulated with dazzling zest, he was never more alien to the Symbolist attitude than when he dictated such a prohibition as this: 'En fait de rythmes, se défier absolument de tout ce qu'on a prétendu inventer depuis le seizième siècle.'

Accepting the liberties secured by Hugo as the *ne plus ultra*, Banville was a reformer only in aspiration. Contrast the attitude of Mallarmé, who adored Banville's poetry, but who felt how disconcerted the French reader must be to have his habits inter-rupted by the death of Victor Hugo. No sooner has the 'giant blacksmith' disappeared than the instrument he had forged breaks in pieces. The whole language recovers its vital rhythms and with them something like the 'manifold cries' of verbal orchestration. That is what the change dates from, though it had been un-deliberately prepared by Verlaine, 'si fluide, revenu à de primi-tives épellations'.[1]

Paul Verlaine occupies a singular place in the development of modern French poetry. Without destroying the mould of the alexandrine, he went further than any of his predecessors in adapting French verse to the fluctuations and nuances of the vaguer emotions. Yet while he broke with the fixity of the Parnassian *maîtrise* and created a fresh and fluent versification,

[1] *Divagations: Crise de Vers.*

he clung to the conviction that, with the latter, he had reached the limits of verse development.

It was after his association with Rimbaud that changes became apparent in Verlaine's technique. The greater number of Rimbaud's poems are, like Verlaine's, written in *vers libérés*. But most of the *Illuminations* are prose-poems interspersed with examples of verse, some of which are as free as any invented since he wrote. To these Verlaine refers as 'prodiges de ténuité, de flou vrai, de charme presque inappréciable à force d'être grêle et fluet'.

Together the vagrant poets seem to have aimed at undermining the prestige of the alexandrine. They increased the number of verse-forms in use and revived lines of unequal numbers of syllables (*vers impairs*). They attacked the rhythmical unity of the classical verse and surpassed the Romantics in dislocating rhythms, practising enjambment, ignoring the regular fall of the cæsura. They simplified rhyme and tried assonance in its place. They broadened the rule of the alternation of masculine and feminine rhymes by admitting sequences of rhymes of the same sex, and they allowed rhyme between similar sounds spelt differently. All this tended to destroy the regularity of traditional French verse and the type of music that went with it, and to impart mobility, fluidity and a new music of a more uncertain character.[1]

Verlaine's rhythmical novelties appeared first in *Romances sans Paroles* (1874), which M. Martino calls 'un vrai album de spécimens de rythmes poétiques'. But they are specimens of *modification* rather than of innovation. His verse remains basically the old verse in its final stage of disintegration, a *vers libéré*, not a

[1] This paragraph is condensed from M. Pierre Martino's *Parnasse et Symbolisme*, p. 156.

vers libre. Verlaine added to the rhythmical forms in use; he had demolished the traditional rhythm of the alexandrine by multiplying its subdivisions and slurring the cæsura—

Beauté des femmes, *leur* faiblesse et ces mains pâles

—and he had popularized the *vers impair*:

Il faut, voyez-vous, nous pardonner les choses (11).
Tournez, tournez, bons chevaux de bois (9).
Va, chanson, à tire-d'aile (7).

But the general rhythm of his work remains romantic. Like his predecessors he never forgets to count syllables. He condemns a rigid, rhyming system but rarely neglects to rhyme. He has no intention of completely proscribing 'ce bijou d'un sou'. A glance at the famous poem from which this phrase comes will show, not only that it is scrupulously rhymed, but that many of its rhymes are rich:

Que ton vers soit la bonne aventure
Eparse au vent crispé du matin
Qui va fleurant la menthe et le thym. . .
Et tout le reste est littérature.

La rime [he wrote in 1888], n'est pas condamnable, mais seulement l'abus qu'on en fait. Rimez faiblement, assonez si vous voulez, mais rimez ou assonez, pas de vers sans cela.[1]

Liberties such as these, followed by so many reservations, hardly imply a revolutionary spirit. Verlaine, we must remember, was opposed to what he called 'Le Cymbalisme' in theory and practice. So far as form goes, for him 'Symbolisme' implied, as André Barre said, merely a revolt against the rules, classic, romantic or parnassian, which would restrict his domain of inspiration or limit his powers of expression. The only rule was

[1] Quoted by A. Barre, *Le Symbolisme*, p. 188.

to have something to say and to say it with all the simplicity of which one was capable:

Et vive un vers *bien* simple! Autrement c'est la prose.[1]

Whatever was implied by 'un vers *bien* simple', Verlaine could not have meant a *vers libre*. That, probably, was what he meant by 'prose'. The new form, of which he openly disapproved, interested him only as an indication that the younger poets felt themselves hampered by existing forms:

> Que l'ambition du vers libre hante
> De jeunes cerveaux épris de hasards!
> C'est l'ardeur d'une illusion touchante,
> On ne peut que sourire à leurs écarts.[2]

To require so complete a revolution would, he thought, be to deny the innate qualities of French poetry and flood it with barbarous rhythms. On more than one occasion he defined his position with regard to the novelties of the Symbolists in humorously blunt terms:

Où sont-elles, les *nouveautés*? Est-ce que Arthur Rimbaud,— et je ne l'en félicite pas,—n'a pas fait tout cela avant eux? Et même Krysinska! Moi aussi, parbleu, je me suis amusé à faire des blagues, dans le temps! Mais enfin, je n'ai pas la prétention de les imposer en Évangile. Certes, je ne regrette pas mes vers de quatorze pieds; j'ai élargi la discipline du vers, et cela est bon; mais je ne l'ai pas supprimée! Pour qu'il y ait vers, il faut qu'il y ait rythme. A présent on fait des vers à mille pattes! Ça n'est plus des vers, c'est de la prose, quelquefois même ce n'est que du charabia. . . Et surtout *ça n'est pas français*, non, *ça n'est pas français*! On appelle ça des vers rythmiques! Mais nous ne sommes ni des Latins, ni des Grecs, nous autres; nous sommes des Français, sacré nom de Dieu.[3]!

[1] *Bonheur*, XVIII.   [2] *Epigrammes*, II, 2. Quoted by A. Barre, *loc. cit.*
[3] J. Huret, *op. cit.*, p. 69.

One thing implicit in this outburst is specially worth comment. Verlaine obviously believed that a radical distinction separates the French type of versification from those of the classical languages. The former, he thought, had no basic feature corresponding to quantity. This conviction, according to Robert de Souza, reveals a misunderstanding of the essential principle of French verse and prevented Verlaine from taking the final step of creating a *vers libre*. In opposition to the traditional view that French verse has no accent and must therefore rely on a count of syllables, Robert de Souza maintained that it had never ceased to be an accentuated verse, in conformity with its rhythmical origins in Latin and with the nature of the language itself. He was thus able to explain to his own satisfaction why Verlaine—and Moréas—stopped where they did.[1]

More sympathetic than Verlaine to the new form, Mallarmé made no attempt to compete as a reformer of the traditional technique. He approved of Verlaine's freed verse, which in its less hazardous forms is much like his own, and he maintained rhyme as a rhythmical principle. On the whole he favoured the retention of the older versification but diversified *ad infinitum*. Apart from the ambiguous experiment, *Un coup de dés*, his observances show far less freedom than his observations. It had been realized, he explained, that the older verse was not 'the absolute form, unique and unchangeable', but simply a means of making sure to write good verses. Lassitude was being

[1] This point will be discussed later. What de Souza said was: 'On s'explique à présent les limites que ne pouvait franchir l'art de Verlaine dont l'accentuation souvent adorable dépendait des groupes numériques et ne les commandait pas. Verlaine est mort convaincu que le français n'avait pas d'accent. Il l'a écrit dans des vers satiriques que ce pauvre Moréas qui jusqu'à son dernier jour eut la même conviction en partage, citait avec complaisance' (*Du Rythme en Français*, p. 58, 1912).

generally felt through abuse of the 'cadence nationale', the use of which, like that of the flag, should remain exceptional. 'Le vers officiel', he told Huret, 'ne doit servir que dans les moments de crise de l'âme.' Yet, it is clear, he wished to see no absolute breach in external technique between Parnassian and Symbolist practice. Just as the *verslibristes* should reserve the alexandrine for 'full organ' effects, the Parnassians should recognize that the new experiment 'complements' the strict verse they love—'les deux efforts peuvent se compléter'.

An essential document in this discussion is that series of observations and meditations in which Mallarmé analysed the changes through which French verse was passing in his time. One of the most acute and representative of his writings, one of the richest in *aperçus*, yet one of the least difficult, *Crise de vers*[1] resumes his complete attitude as a 'witness' interested, though not participating, in the new freedom, the actuality of which he accepts, apparently without a touch of his accustomed irony, as an acquisition, an absolute break with the tradition, exceptional in the history of versification, but with the reservation, to which he always returns, that the older modes should not be supplanted or abandoned; they must be retained for the noblest of traditional uses. As M. Mondor reminds us: 'Au cours de ses entretiens comme dans sa correspondance, il revient au Vers invinciblement.'[2]

Few revolutions, and Mallarmé compares this one with that of '89, could have had so fair-minded, so courteous a critic, sensitive to developments yet scrupulously disinterested in the distinctions he makes. Here, as wherever else he discriminates, Mallarmé's

---

[1] First published in 1892 in the *National Observer* under the title of 'Vers et Musique en France'. Collected in *Divagations*, p. 239.

[2] H. Mondor, *Vie de Mallarmé*, p. 706.

touch discloses nuances, depths and connections hitherto unperceived. The discussion involves his principal technical preoccupation: the relation of poetry to music. His persistent effort to keep the balance between the claims of experiment and those of the tradition was never more clearly stated than in the following paragraph, written for a discussion which ran in the *Figaro* during the year 1895.

Pour moi, le vers classique—que j'appellerai le *vers officiel*—est la grande nef de cette basilique 'la Poésie française'; le vers libre, lui, édifie les bas-côtés pleins d'attirance, de mystère, de somptuosités rares. Le vers officiel doit demeurer, car il est né de l'âme populaire, il jaillit du sol d'autrefois, il sut s'épanouir en sublimes efflorescences. Mais le vers libre est une belle conquête, il a surgi en révolte de l'Idée contre la banalité du 'convenu' seulement, pour être, qu'il ne s'érige pas en église dissidente, en chapelle solitaire et rivale! Sachons écouter les grandes orgues du vers officiel. . . puis n'oublions pas que l'Art est infini.[1]

And what of Moréas, whose flamboyant manifesto inaugurated the Symbolist movement in September 1886? His contribution to the development of free verse need not detain us. His first collections, *Les Syrtes* and *Cantilènes*, which appeared in 1884 and 1886, were strongly influenced in manner and form by Baudelaire and Verlaine. Novelties occur in the *Pèlerin passionné* (1891). Moréas himself claimed that *Agnès*, one of the pieces included in this volume, was among the earliest to be written in *vers libres*.[2] But his addiction to free verse and his allegiance to Symbolism were brief in duration, while his recantation was so absolute that his claim amounts to little more than the desire, on

---

[1] *Le Figaro*, 3 August 1895. See H. Mondor, *op. cit.* p. 717.
[2] He accused Kahn of having kept unpublished his poem 'en vers nouveaux', *Le Chevalier aux blanches armes*, so as to assure his own priority in *La Vogue*. See H. Mondor, *op. cit.* p. 690.

the part of a poet of various gifts and of considerable vanity, to prove he had figured in the forefront of all the important literary changes of his time. By 1890 he had left the ranks of the Symbolists to found the École Romane, a reactionary movement, in accordance with whose neo-classical programme he produced his best work, *Les Stances* (1889, 1901). These poems show a reversion to sixteenth-century models. 'J'ai abandonné le vers libre', he said in 1905,

m'étant aperçu que ses effets étaient uniquement matériels et ses libertés illusoires. La versification traditionelle a plus de noblesse, plus de sûreté, tout en permettant de varier à l'infini le rythme de la pensée et du sentiment; mais il faut être bon ouvrier.[1]

Verlaine's line, the *vers libéré*, was accepted by many poets up to and even after the year 1886 as more or less their standard medium. It represents not a revolution in versification but what might be called the stage of penultimate dislocation. This stage was admirably characterized and delimited by Remy de Gourmont in the following paragraph:

There is one tangible result in poetry of the Symbolist effort; the break-up of the verse. French verse is no longer written as Sully Prudhomme wrote it. [It was Sully Prudhomme who had said: 'La technique du vers est achevé.'] The cæsura is abolished and only survives by chance or habit in view of a particular effect. An exact number of syllables is no longer necessary to the measure of the verse, the mutes count or not according to the musical design. Rich rhyme seems to belong to parody; no one takes this 'bijou d'un sou' seriously; to our ears, which are tired or too refined to enjoy brazen sound, verses *à la* Banville seem constructed upon laborious rhyme-endings. Even simple assonance satisfies us better, and we are more charmed by the surprise produced by sounds that are slightly dissimilar than by the noisy concordance

[1] Le Cardonnel et Vellay: *La Littérature contemporaine* (1905), p.38.

of cymbal-clashing rhymes. Finally the division of rhyme into masculine and feminine seems to us a puerile phonetic heresy; *meurt* and *heure* are excellent rhymes which will shock no one tomorrow. Parnassian versification is as far from us as Latin versification.

Then the critic adds this significant remark: 'I make no allusion here to the *vers libre*, although it is much in favour; it doesn't satisfy me.'[1]

---

[1] *Promenades littéraires*, 4ᵉ série, p. 90.

CHAPTER VII

THE FIRST THEORY OF THE *VERS LIBRE*

I

THE culminating point in the evolution of Symbolism was, in Gustave Kahn's view, the production of the *vers libre*. Kahn was entitled to express an opinion on the matter. Whether or not he was the first to write *vers libres*, he could justly claim to have been the earliest propagandist for the new form. On one ceremonious occasion he was hailed as the 'libérateur du vers français'.[1] Unfortunately in the course of a long literary existence he persistently claimed to have *invented* the new form. This has made critics reluctant to give him his due, and has obscured the question of origins with much dust of controversy. Other aspirants were prompted to air their rights to the 'invention'. In his *Rapport sur le Mouvement poétique français* (1902), Catulle Mendès gave the names of some half-dozen 'originators'. But his ironical remarks on the free-verse movement, for which he had no sympathy, should not be taken seriously. The *vers libre*, he explained, had been advocated in a manual dating from 1880, when a Peruvian exile, Della Rocca de Vergalo, published his *Poétique nouvelle*. Another claim to priority was made on behalf of a Polish Jewess, Mme Marie Krysinska, who maintained that from 1882 to 1883 she had had poems in free verse printed in the *Chat Noir* and other reviews. In his judicious little book, *Les Premiers Poètes du Vers Libre*, Édouard Dujardin points to the fact that this lady's free verses appeared first as fragments of

---

[1] See Remy de Gourmont, *Promenades littéraires*, 4ᵉ série, pp. 65-6.

rhythmical prose and were rearranged and republished in 1890 in a form approximating typographically to *vers libres*. Kahn, we may note, declared that his own free verse had developed out of experiments in poetic prose, in which he had attempted to interest Mallarmé before 1880. Characteristically he explained the whole movement in the same way, contending that the new form proceeded from the poetic prose of the Romantics and Parnassians, and laying particular stress on the development of a conscious type of prose-poem from Aloïsius Bertrand to Baudelaire. In one of Baudelaire's pieces, *Les Bienfaits de la Lune*, he thought the type had been realized to perfection. Some of his own prose-poems had appeared as early as 1879-80, before his departure on military service to Algeria. Returning to Paris in 1885, he took over *La Vogue*, one of the little reviews, which set out on its brief but illustrious course in April of the following year. The first of his *vers libres* to appear in print came in that review for 28 June 1886. These with other *vers libres*, *vers libérés*, and regular verses were collected and published as *Les Palais nomades* in 1887.

Most of the Symbolists were content to accept this work at its author's estimate, as 'le livre d'origine du vers libre'. Dujardin, however, questions the claims of Kahn to absolute priority. He maintains that the very first free verses to appear in *La Vogue* were none of Kahn's experiments. In the course of 1886 the review had produced Rimbaud's *Illuminations*, most of which, it will be remembered, are pieces of poetic prose. A few, however, are more definitely rhythmical, and one of these called *Marine* (published in *La Vogue* for 29 May) Dujardin salutes as 'les premiers vers libres qui aient jamais été publiés'.[1] This is how the piece is presented in editions of Rimbaud's poetry:

[1] *Les Premiers Poètes du Vers Libre* (Paris, 1922), p. 29.

Les chars d'argent et de cuivre,
Les proues d'acier et d'argent
Battent l'écume,
Soulèvent les souches des ronces.

Les courants de la lande
Et les ornières immenses du reflux
Filent circulairement vers l'est,
Vers les piliers de la forêt,
Vers les fûts de la jetée,
Dont l'angle est heurté par des tourbillons de lumière.

Its arrangement in *La Vogue* suggests that it was taken for prose. But the editors seem to have had no doubt about the nature of another of Rimbaud's 'free' poems called *Mouvement*, which came out in the issue for 21 June. It was left to Dujardin to establish the priority of these pieces. Kahn himself never allowed the claim on Rimbaud's behalf and rejected it without discussion in the preface he wrote for a collected edition of his own early poems.[1] It was in the number for 28 June that his own *vers libres* began to appear in the course of a series of poems called *Intermède*, which ran through several numbers of the review.

One more fact in connection with the role of *La Vogue*. The number for 28 June also contained the first of a few translations from Whitman's *Leaves of Grass*. They were made by Jules Laforgue, who had been introduced to the originals by Francis Vielé-Griffin. Dujardin is not the only critic who considers that the form of these translations may have had some influence on the *vers libre*.

It would not have seemed necessary to go further into this question but for the contribution of one other poet, who, with

---

[1] *Premiers Poèmes avec une préface sur le vers libre: Les Palais nomades— Chansons d'Amant— Domaine de Fée* (Paris, 1897).

the exception of Rimbaud, was by far the most original of the early *verslibristes*. This was Jules Laforgue himself. Laforgue's personal development brought him independently to a freer form, the characteristics and differentiæ of which were appreciated by Kahn, who was his friend, in a notable paragraph of the preface to the *Premiers Poèmes*. There Kahn discriminates between his own 'musical' objective and Laforgue's aim—to annotate his sensations as directly, as acutely as possible, without 'chevilles' or conventional embarrassments of any kind. The paragraph is worth quoting:

Laforgue, depuis nos vingt ans simultanés, connaissait mes théories; mais à l'application de mes principes encore embryonnaires, désirs plus que système, mais contenant en germe les développements à venir, nos vers furent bien différents de par nos organisations et nos buts dissemblables. Dans un affranchissement du vers, je cherchais une musique plus complexe, et Laforgue s'inquiétait d'un mode de donner la sensation même, la vérité plus stricte, plus lacée, sans chevilles aucunes, avec le plus d'acuité possible et le plus d'accent personnel, comme parlé. Quoiqu'il y ait beaucoup de mélodie dans les complaintes, Laforgue, se souciant moins de musique (sauf pour évoquer quelque ancien refrain de la rue), négligeait de parti-pris l'unité strophe, ce qui causa que beaucoup de ses poèmes parurent relever, avec des rythmes neufs à foison, et tant de beautés, de l'école qui tendait seulement à sensibiliser le vers, soit celle de Verlaine, Rimbaud et quelques poètes épris de questions de césure, doués dans la recherche d'un vocabulaire rare et renouvelé. Je crois que dès ce moment, et à ce moment (surtout), mes efforts portèrent surtout sur la construction de la strophe, et Laforgue s'en écartait délibérément, volontairement, vers une liberté idéologique plus grande qui le devait conduire à cette phrase mobile et transparente, poétique certes, des poignantes *Fleurs de bonne volonté*.

The insinuation that Rimbaud and Laforgue were connected

with a 'school' that tended merely to 'sensitize' verse is typical of Kahn's condescension. Otherwise the drift of his argument, that Laforgue was aiming at a psychological, not at a musical, mode of expression, is corroborated by Dujardin. As Laforgue's work is so much more interesting and important than Kahn's, let us glance at the stages of its development.

His first volume, *Les Complaintes*, appeared in 1885; another, *L'Imitation de Notre Dame la Lune*, early in 1886. Both were in *vers libérés*. By this time a third volume, *Les Fleurs de bonne Volonté*, was ready for the press and a publisher had been found. But Laforgue decided to withdraw the volume and to treat it as a repertory for new poems. From it he took ideas, images and verses which, incorporated with new elements, produced the *Concile Féerique*, a fantasy in dramatic form of about 200 lines. This was published in *La Vogue* during July 1886 and was, like its predecessors, written in *vers libérés*. Finally in *La Vogue* for 16 August came two of his earliest pieces of *vers libres*. They were collected in a posthumous volume of *Derniers Vers*, which must have been composed between the beginning of 1886 and August of the following year, when Laforgue died. Drawing further upon *Les Fleurs de bonne Volonté*, these last poems, a dozen in all, are entirely in *vers libres*.

It is evident that the years 1885-6 were vital in the history of the new form and that they were dominated by the activities of Kahn. But need we believe that he had 'created' the *vers libre?*[1] Édouard Dujardin put the matter neatly when he implied that Kahn reached his form by an original and independent effort, just as Laforgue did about the same time, and as Rimbaud had done

---

[1] 'En créant le vers libre. . . .' This phrase from *Symbolistes et Décadents* (p. 68) reflects Kahn's attitude. Much of his preface to *Les Palais nomades* is vitiated by the same pretension.

fourteen or fifteen years earlier. It may well be asked, if we omit Rimbaud, whose technical contribution failed to impress his contemporaries and was, so far as the new form goes, quantitatively slight, whether the first significant poet to write *vers libre* was not Jules Laforgue.

II

The question of origins is complicated by the contentions that have sprung up around it. A far more difficult matter, intrinsically, is the theoretical conception underlying the innovation. On this a foreigner dare not dogmatize, when native authorities are found to disagree. But there is one question at least that we may profitably discuss: What did the new form mean to the men who first used it?

One of the reasons why definition or even definiteness seems impossible in this discussion is the ambiguous position of the *vers libre*, intermediary between, on one hand, regular verse and the *vers libéré*, and, on the other, rhythmical prose and the *verset* (the form used in non-metrical versions of the Psalms). 'Le vers libre', says Dujardin, 'est l'aboutissement tant du vers régulier que du poème en prose.'[1] Its unusual typographical arrangement shows an effort to distinguish this from other forms. But any attempt to discriminate theoretically between the *vers libre* and other rhythmical forms not written in metre (such as poetic prose or the *verset*) is dogged by the tendency all these forms have to encroach upon one another. As Remy de Gourmont said: ' . . . il semble plus facile de sentir que de définir la nuance qui sépare tels vers libres de telle prose rythmique.'[2] And so the *vers libre* remains negative in principle, not conforming regularly to any single pattern or type, 'polymorphe', as Mallarmé called it. What

[1] *Op. cit.* p. 55.   [2] *L'Esthétique de la langue française*, p. 273.

at least is clear is that the term itself covers a series of approximate varieties.

Actually the new verse was free only in the sense that it had been liberated in intention from the domination of the traditional metres. In practice most of the *verslibristes* proved to be cautious innovators. We may recall that the long period of experimentation with a view to emancipating French versification, which began before the Romanticists and was thought to have reached its goal with Hugo's liberation of the alexandrine, did not stop there. After a temporary reversion for which the Parnassians were responsible, the mood for experimentation returned and produced successive phases of greater freedom or variety, based on the personal taste or requirement of the poet. The *vers libre* is the visible sign of this flight from traditional conformity. It is the most obvious expression in technique of a movement whose essential spirit or motive has been characterized as individualism. And it is therefore to individual poets of the period that we must look, not for a satisfactory definition of *verslibrisme*, but for a personal account of their own aims and experiments. Among such theorists Gustave Kahn is one of the earliest—probably, as as he claimed, the first. His attempts to explain the new form comprise an article published in 1888 in answer to Brunetière (collected in *Symbolistes et Décadents*), a letter included in one of Huret's interviews and the preface of 1897, which appropriates much from the previous pieces in a larger *vue d'ensemble*.

Kahn interviewed by Huret gave an exhibition of flamboyant egoism, stimulated, no doubt, by a repast with mixed drinks at the reporter's expense. The relevant part of the letter included in the account provides an epitome of the later argument. Having defined a poem as the complete evocation of a poetic idea in free verse, Kahn continues:

Qu'est-ce qu'un vers? C'est un arrêt simultané de la pensée et de la forme de la pensée.—Qu'est-ce qu'une strophe? C'est le développement par une phrase en vers d'un point complet de l'idée.—Qu'est-ce qu'un poème? C'est la mise en situation par ces facettes prismatiques, qui sont les strophes, de l'idée tout entière qu'on a voulu évoquer.

Un livre de vers, c'est-à-dire le poème le plus long et le plus complet qu'on puisse se figurer, doit donc présenter un tout homogène éclairant de toutes ses facettes de strophes un courant de sensations poétiques conçu dans une unité . . . .

Kahn's position, and that of every exponent of the *vers libre*, implies a distinction or rather a discrimination between metre and rhythm, metre itself implying a *selection* of rhythms which has become traditional and (for the *verslibriste*) stereotyped. Kahn insists that the true poet's rhythms are always personal. He would not deny that the traditional metres may best suit the requirements of a poet's mood. Much of the early work of the *verslibristes*, much even of *Les Palais nomades*, made greater use of metre than their authors chose to admit. But Kahn's claim amounts to this, that the modern poet has the right to discard the accepted metres for other rhythms which have not so far been recognised and which resist classification on former prosodical lines. Since moreover he believes that every poet has a rhythm of his own, he looks for a personal rhythm in the verse of Racine. For him the essential rhythm of the first two lines of *Athalie* is represented by the following syllabic groups:

Oui je viens | dans son templ | e adorer | l'Éternel;
Je viens | selon l'usage | antiqu | e et solennel.

This he offers as sufficient scansion, ignoring the cæsura, as (according to him) the masters of classical poetry ignored it, and implying that Racine's verse is based, not on the count of syllables, but on units of free personal rhythm. 'C'est selon notre théorie que ses vers doivent se scander,' he asserts disarmingly. Like all French apologists for literary and artistic novelties, Kahn is here attempting to relate an innovation to the tradition and to assimilate the *vers libre* to the great fixed form by revealing their fundamental identity.

But why has this fundamental element in French versification not been brought out before? The mistake made by both classical and romantic prosodists was that they failed to recognize the *basic unit* of French verse. This is defined in the preface to the *Premiers Poèmes* as 'un fragment le plus court possible figurant un arrêt de voix et un arrêt de sens'—which might be translated as 'the shortest possible fragment corresponding to a pause in reading aloud and in the sense'. How are these units to be assembled and given the cohesion necessary to make a verse? By means of alliteration and assonance, thus:

Des mirages | de leur visage | garde | le lac | de mes yeux.

—a verse which, its author claims, has its own interior existence. But Kahn's concern is not with the verse so much as with the strophe. His predominant interest is apparent in the passage quoted earler, where he distinguishes his method from Laforgue's. The kind of strophe he aimed at was distinct from traditional stanza forms. These are based on a correspondence of metrical lines arranged in a sequence or pattern which recurs regularly. Kahn's strophe is a *logical construction of verse units* developing the principal idea.[1] 'The importance of this technique', he points

[1] Kahn sets his own problem and answers it thus: 'Comment l'apparenter à d'autres vers? Par la construction logique de la strophe, se constituant d'après les mesures intérieures du vers qui dans cette strophe contient la pensée principale ou le point essentiel de la pensée.'

out, 'besides giving prominence to certain harmonies hitherto neglected, will be to enable every poet to realize his own type of verse, or rather an original strophe of his own, and to write an individual rhythm, instead of adopting a ready-made uniform which reduces him to being the pupil of some glorified predecessor or other.' '... un rythme absolument personnel', he insists in another place, 'qui soit suffisant pour interpréter ses lyrismes avec l'allure et l'accent qu'il leur juge indispensables.'

'Désormais,' said Albert Mockel, 'c'est le rythme qui va régir le vers.' But rhythm is based on a recurrent element—in English, for instance, on the tonic accent belonging to the word. In French the tonic accent had been thought either not to exist or not to be sufficiently pronounced to permit of an accentual versification. Hence a prosody based on the count of syllables.

This traditional method Kahn abandons in favour of what he calls the 'accent d'impulsion', that is, the stress which a phrase or group of words acquires when spoken; and he appears to assume that all Frenchmen would distribute the stress in the same way. For Kahn this 'accent of emphasis'[1] is the rhythmical basis for the new versification. He describes its function as 'governing the harmony of the principal verse of the strophe or of an initial verse which gives the movement and on which the other verses will model themselves, except for purposes of contrast'.

Another point on which *verslibristes* have views of their own —often contradictory views—is the mute *e*. Kahn invariably scanned the mute *e*, because, he claimed, it is always, though only faintly, audible.

Rhyme must be modified and rhyming for the eye abandoned. It should not be proscribed but liberated. The clash of cymbals

---

[1] Other exponents, he admits, like Mockel and R. de Souza, call it 'l'accent oratoire'.

at the end of lines (as in Parnassian *rime riche*) must be avoided. Rhyme may be used internally in the verse or it may alternate with assonance, the principle of these changes being that, like the verse itself, rhyme must be mobile. For the same reason there should be no *codified* strophe.

Lines of more than twelve syllables are allowed, so long as the verse is not stretched to the length of a *verset*. The poet's taste and ear will prevent that. He may, however, bring three or four elements together into a single verse, when he wishes to tighten up their effect. Such a verse will wind up the strophe as does the last line in *terza rima*.

III

So far we have dealt with Kahn's personal interpretation of the principles of the new form. As a practical theory it seems to have had no prominence or authority. In the nature of the case it is unlikely that any single theory could be accepted as authoritative. As a general apology for, and explanation of, the *vers libre*, it is vague and sketchy, especially in matters of detail. But its underlying principles—the rejection of the count of syllables, the recognition of some kind of accent and of a 'grammatical' unit of rhythm—have been recognised by other theorists. 'C'est l'*analyse logique* qui détermine les limites du vers moderne,' wrote Albert Mockel. 'La proposition grammaticale coïncide avec le vers, ou, plus souvent, les membres de chaque proposition sont présentés séparément.'[1]

Robert de Souza rejected this idea of a versification based on grammatical units. For him French verse was accentual—a fact unperceived until disclosed by Rousselot's phonetic apparatus.

---

[1] *Propos de Littérature*, p. 83.

'Le vers n'est plus l'unité fondamentale qui nous importe', he said, 'mais le *pied rythmique*, dont dépend la nature du mouvement et dont relève déjà celle de nos mètres classiques.'[1]

Dujardin approved of Kahn's definition, but referred to his conception of the *vers libre* as 'une sorte de pied rythmique supérieur'. This kind of foot, he maintained, is the basis of all forms of French versification. It was ignored by Classical and Romantic prosodists in favour of the count of syllables, to which even the *vers libéré* of Verlaine conforms. The new form breaks absolutely with this practice: 'Le vers libre ne modifie pas, il *ignore* le nombre des syllabes.' And Dujardin suggests that the two systems could best be distinguished by the terms 'vers syllabique' and 'vers non-syllabique'.[2]

One more reaction is worth indicating. In a critical discussion of Kahn's theory Remy de Gourmont defined the new verse in his own way:

Le vrai vers libre est conçu comme tel, c'est-à-dire comme fragment musical dessiné sur le modèle de son idée émotive, et non plus déterminé par la loi fixe du nombre.[3]

The value of Kahn's theory is that it shows how one of the most prominent of early *verslibristes* conceived of his own experiment. Where he, in company with other theorists, lays the stress is on *rhythm*, on the desire to present the poem so as to bring out the personal sense of rhythm at the expense of all other modes, however venerable, which are felt as obstructions to the impulse.

Such a programme might appear to offer a field for open competition in poet's licence. Yet the result, as seen in the poetry

[1] *Du Rythme en Français*, p. 21.

[2] *Op. cit.* p. 14.

[3] *L'Esthétique de la langue française: Le Vers Libre*, p. 251. This piece is a critical commentary on the theory and practice of Kahn.

of the late 'eighties and 'nineties, though it may once have looked anarchical, can hardly at this time be called chaotic. The *vers-libristes* turned out to be far less audacious in practice than in theory, and more respectful of traditional forms than they had threatened to be.[1] One may ask whether Kahn's work itself shows much rhythmical variety, at least in his first volume. It may be useful to conclude with a glance at its formal elements.

Les Palais nomades are in eight sections bearing sub-titles. The first two sections present no striking novelties of form. A musical conception predominates, Section I being called 'Thème et variations'. The theme is a kind of introduction in rhythmical prose, printed in italics. But the ten poems that follow are in regular verse. A similar arrangement holds for the 'Mélopées' of Section II. In his preface of 1897 Kahn explained this disposition as due to a comparison of the 'rhythmical parts' of Baudelaire's *Fleurs du Mal* and *Poèmes en prose*, which gave him the idea of a mixed production—'un livre mixte où les deux formes de phrases

---

[1] Distinguishing between those whose work was truly rhythmical and those whose limited experiments were based on the count of syllables, Robert de Souza concluded thus on the question of origins:

'En se remémorant la double source extérieure de notre composition rythmique, née, pour l'origine contemporaine immédiate, du poème en prose de Baudelaire, puis de la prose métrique de Villiers de l'Isle Adam et de Mallarmé, en même temps que du vers multiple ou fluide de Verlaine, dernier stade de l'évolution historique apparente, la chaîne des véritables rythmeurs, avant 1900, n'a pas d'autres maillons que ceux-ci: Arthur Rimbaud (*La Saison en Enfer*), Jules Laforgue, Gustave Kahn, Francis Vielé-Griffin, Maurice Maeterlinck (*Chansons*, dialogues dramatiques, prose rythmée), Albert Mockel, Charles van Leberghe, Paul Claudel (*Drames*, prose métrique), Jean Thorel (*Promenades sentimentales*, prose rythmée et métrique), André Gide (*Les Nourritures terrestres*, prose rythmique), Tristan Leclère (Klingsor), Henri Ghéon.' (*Du Rythme en Français*, p. 48.)

Souza excludes Moréas, Henri de Régnier and Verhaeren from among the 'rythmiciens'. The first two were 'parnassiens-nés', the latter was a Romantic. All three were satisfied with new manipulations of the older measures.

chantées eussent logiquement alterné'. Dujardin considers that *vers libres* begin to appear in the third section, *Intermède*. This section seems to be transitional and not much in advance of the first; the verse shows no persistent irregularities. What gives an air of basic regularity to most of Kahn's poems, keeping them, as it were, in touch with the tradition, is his admitted preoccupation with the strophe. Despite all variations his typical poem has the appearance of being dominated by 'stanza form', though treated with much liberty. Such a pattern, it may be noted, was used by other poets in the late 'eighties as a transitional mode leading to greater freedom.[1] It is only in the last two sections of Kahn's first volume, *Mémorial* and *Finale*, that we find an irregularity of form which escapes all possibilities of comparison with, for instance, the *vers libres* of La Fontaine. Here is an example:

C'est vers ta chimère
Vers les gonfalons et les pennons de ta chimère
Que vont les désirs en pieux pèlerins—
Pèlerins fatigués de rhythmes obsesseurs
Reposez-vous à l'ombre acquise
A l'ombre apaisée dormez les sommeils berceurs des haltes.

(Lieds)

The two later collections included in *Les Premiers Poèmes*— *Chansons d'Amant* and *Domaine de Fée*—show much more rhythmical freedom, though the strophic arrangement persists. But they date respectively from 1891 and 1895, when *vers libres* of the most audacious type had ceased to be a novelty. In content and feeling most of these pieces are moods of facile melancholy or evocation, full of echoes and recurrences without much significance. *File à ton rouet . . .* is found in many anthologies. Its lilt is not without charm but shows no great originality. The only

---

[1] See chap. VI, 'The Transition in Technique', in my book, *Emile Verhaeren* (1926).

value Kahn's poems are likely to retain is historical, as early experiments in rhythm.

It may be worth recording that in the winter of 1913-14 the writer had the privilege of a talk with Gustave Kahn, mainly concerning the *vers libre*. About a dozen years earlier, in the course of a Congress of Poets held at Paris, some of the younger men had called for Kahn's head as a protest against his partialities. These were not much in evidence on the afternoon of my visit. His manner was direct, helpful and subdued. He rejected the suggestion that the *vers libre* was an innovation: it was a 'logical development'. He caught at the idea that it proceeded from poetic prose and repeated the thesis of its development from Baudelaire, citing some of his own early efforts in the *Revue Moderne et Naturaliste* (1879-80). Of a possible contribution from Rimbaud he would hear nothing. These were clearly convictions. The impression he gave was one of wide practical knowledge of the movement to which he had belonged. His activities as editor, historian and critic *de la première heure*, cannot, of course, be denied and, as for the priority he assumed, it seems clear that he must at least have been the first to publish a developed account of the nature of the new verse. No verdict could approach finality without more detailed and extensive considerations. The contribution of Vielé-Griffin, for instance, and the campaign he waged from 1890 in *Les Entretiens politiques et littéraires* would have to be estimated.[1] A tentative conclusion might be borrowed from Remy de Gourmont, who was a close, if not an enthusiastic, observer of the development. Professing to have no wish to revive old quarrels, he asserted, in an article on Kahn, that both the theory and the most decisive examples of

[1] His first free verse appeared in *Joies* (1889); the preface to this collection begins with the declaration: 'Le vers est libre.'

the new versification belonged to the author of *Les Palais nomades*.[1] A few years earlier, one is tempted to recall, the same critic, while expressing a doubt whether the new verse was 'fait pour nos climats', had invidiously added that the inventor of new tools is not usually the man who applies them on masterpieces.[2]

[1] *Promenades littéraires*, 4ᵉ série, pp. 65, 66.
[2] *Ibid.*, 1ᵉ série, p. 238.

CHAPTER VIII

WHITMAN AND THE ORIGINS OF
THE *VERS LIBRE*

I

THE question of the origins of the *vers libre* has been obscured
by a number of partial solutions. Of these the persistent
claims made by Gustave Kahn to priority in the invention have
provoked suspicions which investigation has done nothing to
remove; they suggest by opposition the right to consideration
of other experimenters of lesser egoism and greater originality.
But the question cannot really be settled without taking into
account another suggestion of a different order, namely that
modern French free verse owes its origins partly, if not primarily,
to foreign influence. It is a fact that a large number of the early
verslibristes were of foreign extraction. 'Je remarque avec assez
d'étonnement,' said Heredia, 'que ce sont des Belges, des Suisses,
des Grecs, des Anglais et des Américains qui veulent renouveler
le vers français.' Francis Vielé-Griffin, one of the leading pro-
tagonists for the new form and perhaps its most consistent
practitioner, was an American by birth, and many of his com-
panions in the Symbolist campaign admired the freedom and
flexibility of English and German versifications. It has even been
maintained that the free, line-for-line renderings it was customary
to make from foreign poets gave an impulse to new ventures in
French prosody.

In this connection Whitman's name has been cited and the
possibility of a formative influence exerted by *Leaves of Grass* on
the *vers libre* has been hinted or asserted by several critics. One

of the earliest statements of this kind came from that prominent exponent of Symbolism, Remy de Gourmont: 'A qui doit-on le vers libre? . . . surtout à Walt Whitman dont on commençait alors à goûter la licence majestueuse.'[1] In a book on the Symbolists published in 1900, an American, Vance Thompson, went one better: 'And just as Poe created modern French prose, Whitman re-created modern French verse.'[2] Four years later Remy de Gourmont repeated his implication, though in less definite terms: 'On traduisit également vers 1883 quelques poèmes de Walt Whitman, dont la libre rythmique ne fut pas sans influence sur le mouvement symboliste et la création du vers libre.'[3] In the same year Émile Blémont wrote with unaccountable conviction:

De cette époque date l'action incontestable de Walt Whitman sur le mouvement poétique qui se développa en France au déclin du dernier siècle; car on peut affirmer que l'auteur des *Brins d'Herbe* exerça sur les 'Verslibristes' et autres groupes émancipateurs une influence analogue, mais diamétralement contraire à celle qu'avait exercée Edgar Poe sur les Parnassiens.[4]

With these assertions of men on the spot, who may have lacked the advantage of perspective, let us compare a similar suggestion which the most popular anthology of Symbolist poetry, *Les Poètes d'Aujourd'hui*, has allowed to stand in its introduction to the selection of Kahn's poems. With reference to the claims made by, or on behalf of, certain 'originators', we read:

C'est là une question qui n'est pas encore bien tranchée, et le vers libre, en admettant qu'il n'ait pas toujours existé plus ou moins, n'a peut-être été, tout d'abord, sous sa forme actuelle,

---

[1] *Le Livre des Masques*, p. 245.
[2] Vance Thompson, *French Portraits*.
[3] *Promenades littéraires*, 1e série, *La littérature anglaise en France*, p. 327.
[4] Émile Blémont, *Beautés étrangères*, postcript.

qu'un des résultats de l'influence de poètes étrangers, notamment du poète américain, Walt Whitman, très apprécié des écrivains symbolistes.[1]

Assumptions of literary influence frequently thrive on such vague insinuations; and this specimen has had thirty years' incubation. Actually the main implication of the paragraph was explained away in an interview I had early in 1914 with one of the joint compilers of the anthology. A contemporary of the movement and an editor of repute, Van Bever ridiculed the notion of Whitmanian influence and appeared astonished when shown the passage in question, for the editing and innuendoes of which he contrived to make his colleague, Paul Léautaud, responsible. The other statements appear to be no more substantial. At best they are expressions of opinion, unsupported by explanation or proof. Remy de Gourmont, to whom I wrote on the matter, referred me to Vielé-Griffin as being the most likely person to furnish the true solution.

II

It was Vielé-Griffin who had introduced Whitman's work to Laforgue and had published several translations from the *Leaves*. His first collection of *vers libres* came out in 1889. Three years later, on the death of Whitman, he referred to the form, 'ô absolument libre, du poète des *Brins d'Herbe*'.[2] But when questioned early in 1914, he not only denied any debt to Whitman, but rejected the suggestion that *Leaves of Grass* could have had any influence whatsoever on the origins of French free verse. This, he maintained, was a native development proceeding from the *vers*

[1] Van Bever et Léautaud, *Poètes d'Aujourd'hui*, I, p. 203.
[2] *Entretiens politiques et littéraires*, April 1892; *Autobiographie de Walt Whitman*.

libéré of Verlaine. Until lately, he thought, Whitman had had no effect on poets of the French tongue, with the possible exceptions of Maeterlinck and Claudel. To them we shall refer later; let us first consider the case of Jules Laforgue.

Laforgue, as we have seen, had translated some of the *Leaves*, his renderings appearing in numbers of *La Vogue* from 28 June to 2 August 1886. They comprised eight of the *Inscriptions* along with *O Star of France* and *A Woman Waits for me*. In July *La Vogue* published the last of his own *vers libérés* (*Le Concile féerique*), while the number for 16 August contained the first of his *vers libres*. M. F. Strowski once referred to Laforgue as having 'appris de l'Américain, Walt Whitman, ce qu'une oreille naturellement musicale avait enseigné à Marie Krysinska'.[1] This need not be taken too seriously. But one may reasonably ask whether Whitman's example could have effected the eleventh-hour transformation in Laforgue's technique. Téodor de Wyzewa, in the article already quoted, described Laforgue, at the end of his short life, as a tireless reader of Whitman; but he denied the possibility of influence. Probably the only person who could have spoken with authority on the matter was the late Édouard Dujardin, author of that invaluable little book, *Les Premiers Poètes du Vers Libre*. There he admitted having discussed points of technique with Laforgue in Berlin before the translations were published, but he could recall no reference to the American poet and found nothing on the subject in the correspondence.[2]

A more useful question raised by Dujardin is that of the possible role of Laforgue's translations in determining the type of the first *vers libres*. Pointing to the 'family connection' between the *verset* and the *vers libre*, he sees no objection to including the

[1] F. Strowski, *La Littérature française du XIXe siècle*, p. 458.
[2] *Op. cit.*, p. 59.

'verset Whitmanien' in a history of the origins of the *vers libre*.[1] He admits that attempts, before Laforgue's, were made to translate some of the *Leaves*, but these he considers of no formal interest. The question is, how near do Laforgue's translations keep to the *form* of Whitman's poems? Dujardin confesses that he has not compared the renderings with the originals, but affirms that their form is precisely that which the *vers libre* (or the *verset*) was then acquiring: 'S'ils avaient été publiés sans nom d'auteur, ces poèmes auraient été des vers libres (ou des versets), et voilà qui me semble considérable.'

His omission is all the more regrettable because of the difficulty of consulting a review so rare as *La Vogue*. An indirect means of comparison is, however, available, which we may regard as practically, if not absolutely, reliable. In 1918 appeared a selection of Whitman's poems translated by half a dozen French writers of distinction and incorporating the original translations of Laforgue.[2] It seems reasonable to assume that the form in which his translations are reproduced in this edition (the aim of which was to improve on Bazalgette's) is identical with that which they had

---

[1] *Op. cit.* p. 49. This assimilation of the *vers libre* to the *verset* seems to me questionable. Kahn would have none of it. And yet it is possible that the *verset biblique* played a certain role in this development. Reviewing the first edition of *Poètes d'Aujourd'hui* in 1900, Remy de Gourmont estimated the extent of foreign influence in these words: 'D'abord l'Amérique, par Edgar Poe, dont Stéphane Mallarmé renouvela les poèmes, et surtout par Walt Whitman que nous firent connaître quelques traductions de Jules Laforgue et de M. Francis Vielé-Griffin. Le vers libre, tel que le comprend ce dernier poète, vient en partie de Whitman; mais Whitman était lui-même un fils de la Bible et ainsi le vers libre, ce n'est, peut-être, au fond, que le verset hébraïque des prophètes: c'est bien également de la Bible, mais de la Bible allemande, cette fois, que semble nous venir une autre nuance du vers libre, celle qui a valu sa réputation à M. Gustave Kahn. Mais M. Kahn n'est biblique que de forme; M. Vielé-Griffin l'est aussi d'intelligence et de cœur ....' (*Le Problème du Style*, pp. 158-9).

[2] *Walt Whitman: Œuvres choisies*, N.R.F., 1918.

in *La Vogue*. After comparing them with Whitman's poems, one is at least able to affirm that Laforgue's renderings, as printed in the selection of 1918, are almost perfectly literal both verbally and formally. Here and there the French seems to lack the character of the English. For instance, the phrase 'her athletic democracy' has a typical epithet, the force of which is lost in 'sa puissante démocratie', and the line:

> But you, ye untried latencies, will thrill to every page,

is diluted to:

Mais à chaque page vous allez tressaillir de choses qu'on n'a pas dites.

Such deficiencies, however, are rare; and but for one slight difference, Whitman's form seems scrupulously followed. His habit of grouping lines in paragraphs or sections, even in his shorter pieces, is practically ignored by Laforgue—possibly to economise space in a diminutive review. Only the rendering of *O Star of France* makes any attempt to repeat this feature. But this inobservance has no effect on the *rendering of the line*, which imitates Whitman's as closely as possible. And it is of the line in Laforgue's translations that Dujardin is evidently thinking when he says they might have suggested to a young French poet the idea of the *vers libre* or of the *verset*. The same, he thinks, holds true of Vielé-Griffin's translations, some of which appeared in 1888. But actual proof of their effect is lacking. Whether these renderings from the *Leaves* exerted any immediate influence on the form of the new experiments in French versification will probably always remain a matter of speculation, if indeed the question is thought to be worth more attention. Dujardin's views are at least a proof that such speculations continued to be indulged in up to 1922.

My own conclusions, reached earlier, were negative.

In short [runs an article of 1916], had not fragments of Whitman's poetry been translated about the time when the first *vers libres* were being written, probably no attempt would have been made to forge a link connecting the two phenomena. That the amorphous rhapsodies of the American are much more unbridled than the freest French verses of that time is unconsciously demonstrated in the pages of the *Revue Indépendante* for 1888, where some of the earliest *vers libres* are printed alongside renderings of *Leaves of Grass*.[1]

Today I remind myself that epithets like 'amorphous', 'unbridled' and 'lawless' can be too freely applied to Whitman's verse. Mr Hugh I'Anson Fausset pointed out recently that Whitman himself described it 'as apparently lawless, but on closer examination a certain regularity appears, like the recurrence of lesser and longer waves on the seashore, rolling without intermission, and fitfully rising and falling'. And Mr Fausset adds: 'What held his verse together, however loosely, and enabled it to carry in an unbroken current, cargoes of facts and prose-statements, was a force of measured declamation.'[2] It is the declamatory nature of Whitman's verse which distinguishes it most radically from the poetry of the Symbolists.

III

Further confirmation in a negative sense—but with an interesting reservation on the positive side—will be found in a book on Maeterlinck by Mr Jethro Bithell. Discussing the question of the origin of *vers libres*, he writes:

[1] 'Influence of Walt Whitman on the origin of the *Vers Libre*', *Mod. Lang. Rev.*, April 1916.

[2] *Walt Whitman, Poet of Democracy* (1942), pp. 131, 132.

As for Walt Whitman and Vielé-Griffin, it is true that translations had appeared, but they had not attracted the least notice, and no one betrayed the slightest interest for the technique of the American poet. As a matter of fact, few people knew anything about Whitman, beside the two poets of American birth, Francis Vielé-Griffin and Stuart Merrill; and both at that time, although of course their manner was new, were writing, so far as *form* is concerned, *regular* verses.[1]

Mr Bithell then turns to the connection between Whitman and the Belgian poets, and in doing so presents what is possibly the first definite case of Whitman's influence on French poetry:

Another of the first poets to write free verses, the Walloon poet, Albert Mockel, was not unacquainted with Whitman; he had read *American Poems, selected by William M. Rossetti.* Now Mockel, as editor of *La Wallonie,* which he had founded to defend the new style, was connected with the whole group of symbolists and *verslibristes,* all of whom, practically, were regular contributors to the review ... But as it happened, Mockel was not in the least inspired by the selections from Whitman in Rossetti's collection; they made the impression on him of being Bible verses rather than real verses. One poet Whitman's lawless line did directly influence; and this was Maeterlinck, whose rhymeless verse in *Serres Chaudes* was written under the inspiration of *Leaves of Grass.* But *Serres Chaudes* did not appear till 1889, and even then the majority of the poems in the volume were rhymed and regular; so that it could hardly be claimed that Maeterlinck was the originator of the *vers libre.*[2]

The authority for these assertions was, Mr Bithell informed me, a written statement received from Albert Mockel. An examination of certain pieces in *Serres Chaudes* will show how

---

[1] Jethro Bithell, *Maurice Maeterlinck* ('Great Writers', 1913?).

[2] Mr Bithell adds in a footnote: 'He himself told Huret that *La Princesse Maleine* was written in *vers libres* concealed typographically as prose.'

plausible the contention is. Most of the poems in this small volume are written in octosyllabic quatrains. But interspersed are seven longer pieces without rhyme or metre. In this they are at once ahead of the freest *vers libres* of that time, and abreast of Whitman's emancipated lines, to which indeed they bear more than one striking resemblance. Whitman's mode of writing has been called the 'catalogue style', though this is a rough characterization. Many of his pieces consist of a series of impressions set down in rapid succession, as if to give a sense of cinematographic continuity. In others the peculiar flavour or nuance of an emotional experience may be suggested by means of a sequence of approximate references or allusions.

It is curious to note—developing a hint from Mr Bithell[1]— how near this mode comes to what has been distinguished by more than one exponent of Symbolism as the characteristic method of the school. In his book, *L'Attitude du Lyrisme contemporain*, Tancrède de Visan wrote, by way of definition, 'Le symbolisme . . . se sert d'images successives ou accumulées pour extérioriser une intuition lyrique.' And it was to the dramas and poems of Maeterlinck that he turned for the best illustrations of this technique: 'Nous le voyons dans *Serres Chaudes* entasser à dessein les images pour mieux nous faire pénétrer son impression subtile.'[2]

In the 'free' poems of *Serres Chaudes* an attempt is made to communicate an *état d'âme* or to suggest what is remote or abstruse by means of a series of concrete references. But these are not the most obvious grounds of comparison. Each case shows an exceptional use of exclamatory devices. Most of the

[1] *Op. cit.* p. 28.
[2] Tancrède de Visan, *op. cit.* p. 120. It should be noted that the author refers in this connection to Bergson and to the Bible, not to Whitman.

typical *Leaves of Grass* are, in form, a sequence of declamatory enumerations, held together by repetitions of initial words or phrases and ending with marks of exclamation. Such devices are at least as old as the litany. What is novel is the systematic reiteration of them in modern poetry. Whitman once referred to his mode of presentation as 'a perpetual series of what might be called *ejaculations*'. And Maeterlinck might have made the same claim:

> O ces regards pauvres et las!
> Et les vôtres et les miens!
> Et ceux qui ne sont plus et ceux qui vont venir!
> Et ceux qui n'arriveront jamais et qui existent cependant!
> Il y en a qui semblent visiter des pauvres un dimanche;
> Il y en a comme des malades sans maison;
> Il y en a comme des agneaux dans une prairie couverte de linges.
>
> Et ces regards insolites!
> Il y en a sous la voûte desquels on assiste à l'exécution d'une vierge dans une salle close,
> Et ceux qui font songer à des tristesses ignorées!
> A des paysans aux fenêtres de l'usine,
> A un jardinier devenu tisserand,
> A une après-midi d'été dans un museé de cires,
> Aux idées d'une reine qui regarde un malade dans le jardin,
> A une odeur de camphre dans la forêt,
> A enfermer une princesse dans une tour, un jour de fête,
> A naviguer toute une semaine sur un canal tiède.

With this may be compared almost any of the longer poems from *Leaves of Grass*, some of which like *Salut au Monde* surpass anything of their kind in superabundance of initial repetition and ejaculation. But nothing Whitman wrote resembles the above passage more closely in substance, as well as in technique and style, than the composition entitled *Faces*. Now this piece was one of two translated by Vielé-Griffin and published in the *Revue Indépendante* in 1888, a year before the appearance of *Serres Chaudes*. Here is a paragraph from the translation:

Flânant par les pavés ou chevauchant par le sentier rustique, ô ces visages!
Visages d'amitié, de précision, de cautèle, de suavité, d'idéal;
Le visage de spirituelle prescience et, toujours bien-venu, le bon visage du vulgaire;
Le visage de qui chante une musique, les majestueux visages des avocats de nature et de juges au large crâne;
Le visage de ceux qui chassent et qui pêchent, aux tempes saillantes, le glabre et pâle visage d'orthodoxes citoyens;
Pur, exalté en désirs, interrogateur, le visage de l'artiste;
Le visage hideux de telle âme belle, le visage beau et qu'on déteste ou qu'on méprise;
Le saint visage de l'enfance, le visage illuminé de la mère d'enfants nombreux;
Le visage d'un amour, le visage d'une vénération;
Le visage comme d'un rêve, le visage d'un roc impassible;
Le visage qui n'exhibe plus bien ni mal, le visage châtré;
Fauve épervier, dont furent rognées les pennes,
Étalon qui dut enfin céder aux pinces et au couteau du châtreur,
Flânant ainsi par les pavés, ou passant le bac qui ne se repose,
des visages et des visages et des visages,
Je les vois et ne me plains pas et suis content de tous.

Here the same devices are used, but for dissimilar purposes. In tone and feeling there is, of course, no parallel. The attenuated languor and mysticity of the modern Fleming's sensibility, as annotated in the 'free' poems of his 'hot-house' collection, fade to a whimper beside the claim Whitman made on behalf of his own technique:

... in this free metre and in verses singularly exhilarating, and that affect one like an atmosphere unusually charged with oxygen, he, by a perpetual series of what might be called *ejaculations*, manages to express himself on about every theme interesting to humanity . . . with illustrations drawn largely from our own times and country.[1]

Of poets connected with the Symbolist movement Paul Claudel is the only one who uses a *verset* which at times comes near to Whitman's in tone as well as in form:

Les mots que j'emploie
Ce sont les mots de tous les jours, et ce ne sont point les mêmes!
Vous ne trouverez point de rimes dans mes vers ni aucun sortilège. Ce sont vos phrases mêmes. Pas aucune de vos phrases que je ne sache reprendre.[2]

Claudel used this form for the *earlier* edition of his play, *Tête d'or*. It appeared in 1890, but was composed in 1889—the year when Maeterlinck's poems were published, the year, too, when Gabriel Sarrazin produced a striking study of Whitman in his *Renaissance de la Poésie Anglaise*. Whitman's name has often been coupled with Claudel's. M. André Gide, with whom I once discussed the matter, seems to have been convinced of Claudel's indebtedness to the *Leaves*. Usually, however, it is the Bible, the dramas of Aeschylus and Shakespeare and Rimbaud's *Illuminations* that are cited as his models. The French poet himself, we should note, claimed to have invented his own form:

J'inventai ce vers qui n'avait ni rime ni mètre,
Et je le définissais dans le secret de mon cœur cette fonction double et réciproque
Par laquelle l'homme absorbe la vie, et restitue, dans l'acte suprême de l'expiration,
Une parole intelligible.[3]

---

[1] Quoted by Hugh I'Anson Fausset, *op. cit.* p. 274.
[2] *La Muse qui est la Grâce.*   [3] *La Ville* (*Théâtre*, II, p. 236).

But the question of priority need not be raised. Claudel's work belongs to a time when Whitman's is becoming better known and cultivated in France, and when the *vers libre* movement has passed beyond the stage of inception with which we are here concerned. So far as this stage goes in its relation to Whitman, our own conclusions must remain tentative.

IV

The *vers libre* might be described as an emancipated form designed to meet the demand felt by certain French poets, towards the end of the nineteenth century, for greater rhythmical freedom and variety than they could derive from regular verse. Its principles were claimed to be innate in French versification from the earliest times, and approximations to the ideal of freedom were perceived in the technique of a succession of experimenters. But as a recognized mode of lyrical expression, the modern *vers libre* dates from the 'eighties, when a definite reaction occurred against the limitations re-imposed on verse by the bronze and marble ideals of Parnassian prosody. In the period that followed, characterized by the interpenetration and co-ordination of the arts, having made music, not sculpture, their extra-literary model, some of the more revolutionary spirits contrived to adapt old forms or to invent others to suit their sensibilities. So far the movement was of purely French origin, the last, in fact, of a series of breaks with the traditional modes. The development, however, may have been affected in some degree by external influences. A more or less intimate acquaintance with foreign prosodies was possessed by some of the innovators, and it is probable that models were sought, or at least perceived, in less rigorous versifications. Such examples would not only guide the innovator but help to legitimatize his venture. He might feel a certain moral support in being able to point to an achievement comparable with what he was aiming at himself. It would at any rate furnish an argument against the critics at home. He might even fall into the error of attaching an exaggerated importance to his foreign prototype. In this way not a few poets have gained abroad posthumous reputations, disproportionate to the rank accorded to them in their native literatures. Neither Poe nor Whitman has escaped this sort of literary lionizing in France.

Of all external influences contributory to the freeing of French verse that of Whitman has been most frequently suggested. It happened that he was himself in a position comparable in some ways to that of the early *verslibristes*. Having adopted a novel and personal form, unfettered by rhyme or metre, he too was suffering from the uncompromising boldness of his innovation at the hands of disconcerted critics reared in the old school. By 1887, the date of the publication of Kahn's first volume of *vers libres*, Whitman had accomplished over thirty-two years' work. *Leaves of Grass* was in its sixth edition. Young French poets, struggling to attain a personal medium, may have been interested to hear of an elder poet engaged in a campaign similar to their own. From America, where Whitman was slowly gaining recognition, had come Vielé-Griffin and Stuart Merrill; and we have seen something of what they did to make Whitman better known in France. But his importance for the French must not be fixed at too early a date. It would be safer to say that when the first *vers libres* were being written, the poets who knew Whitman, and they were few, were attracted mainly through the appeal made by his brusque originality to their pronounced taste for literary novelties. The 'astounding' thing about Whitman was not the way his poems were composed but the man they revealed. His admirers may have regarded him as a foreign master who had achieved a revolution in poetical form bearing some kind of relation to what they were attempting, but they could never have looked up to him as a magician who would initiate them into the mysteries of a startling technical innovation.

This seems as far as our investigations permit us to go, and even here much is conjecture. The question of Whitman's influence raises the larger question of the nature or of the assumption of literary influence in general. Not infrequently the word 'influence' is used as a term of comparison with invidious implications. In saying that one work has been 'influenced' by another, what is often meant is that it is derived or copied. Still more often the word is used loosely to classify or characterize a work by resemblance. To say that certain *verslibristes* were 'influenced' by Whitman's line may simply have meant that, for the observer, the French experimenters had attempted something comparable to what Whitman appeared to have done. The earliest statements about Whitman's influence on the Symbolists and *verslibristes* seem to be of this vague kind—assertions made by critics, essayists and reviewers of standing, but made without any show of evidence or attention to proof. On the other hand, to admit that little demonstrable effect has been discovered where much was implied does not set a limit to inquiry. Quite apart from the possibility of new facts coming to light, there is always the probability that such an influence as may have been exerted by Whitman's example (as it was understood by the Symbolists) operated less through direct contact with his works than by way of 'hints and indirections' (to borrow his words), hints and indirections reacting in ways too subtle and intimate to be caught in the net of such methods as have here been applied.

CHAPTER IX

TALKS WITH FRENCH POETS IN 1913-14

'DON'T go mugging round the Bibliothèque Nationale,' said Mr Ezra Pound as I set out, after my first and only talk with him in the autumn of 1913, on the track of Whitman's influence on modern French poets. His advice turned out to be excellent. I was soon to find that it was difficult at that time to make the big French libraries disgorge anything of importance on the recent poetic movements, and these were still academically taboo. Mr Pound furnished a few addresses of the right people to see when I reached Paris, and, once there, a start was made by calling on M. Georges Duhamel, then domiciled in the popularly picturesque rue Mouffetard. From him I secured a few more addresses, including a coveted note to Verhaeren.

I am afraid I took for granted the responses that awaited my persistent inquiries, tiresome enthusiasms and considerable ignorance. The appeals I made for clues or guidance prompted receptions which, though modest when compared with those of an expert interviewer, have always seemed to me generous. Subsequent efforts have never been able to recapture the vivacity and *bonhomie* of those talks. Not that French literary men have become less hospitable, less affable, since the first World War. Perhaps it is simply that youth makes a better audience than maturity, especially for members of a race with a genius for expansiveness, so often damped by that *froideur*, that *morgue*, which remain the conventional attitude of the seasoned Britisher abroad. But there may be another explanation of the ease with which conversations began. Academic as was the nature of my inquiries, they were hardly remote from the interests of most of my interlocutors. Everyone I met having pretensions to an acquaintance with contemporary poetry was more or less aware of the objects of my quest—Whitman and the *vers libre*. The *vers libre* seemed to be the quarry of every living poet or his *bête noire*. As for Whitman, while each poet denied his influence, few were averse to invoking it in the case of a colleague; though the motive for such implications may have been the wish to help an anxious researcher with a hint for possible copy.

That most fervent of Whitmanites, Léon Bazalgette, had corresponded with me already and urged a trip to Paris. The liveliest feelings of gratitude remain for the interest he took in my efforts, the notes scribbled when a useful idea struck him, the manuscripts lent to fill gaps in my material, above all, the talks we had during office hours or at street corners or in that modest eating-house which, though it faced the Boulevard St Germain, had taken the name of a side-street, calling itself immodestly enough, 'le restaurant du Dragon'. Similar feelings keep fresh in mind the kindness of Tancrède de Visan. If the author of *L'Attitude du Lyrisme Contemporain* should have survived the thirty odd years of chaos that separate our tranquil discussions from the din of present controversies, he could hardly be expected to remember the efforts he would sometimes make on behalf of a student who has not forgotten his appearing in frock coat and top hat, bearing to the fifth storey of an old house in the rue du Vieux Colombier a few numbers of that *rarissime* little review, *La Vogue*, wrapped in a newspaper under his arm; and who also recalls having been introduced by him, after a matinée in the adjacent theatre (then in its prime), to an immaculate figure with a severe visage and a monocle: Robert de Souza, the last word incarnate on the newest fashion in French rhythms.

Another pleasant though fading memory is of a talk or two with the late André Gide, whom I met through an unwitting fraud. A French lady living in England had provided a word of introduction to the poet, M. André Spire. During a protracted search of his address the more important name seems to have supplanted the other in my mind, the confusion persisting until I had called at M. Gide's residence and deposited the card. Late that night I came to my senses and immediately scribbled a couple of apologies. Stern reproaches ensued from the lady across the Channel. But their asperity was softened by a gracious little note that had preceded them from M. Gide himself, pretending he was pleased with my blunder and responding to my request for information. We met briefly once or twice. I was struck by his extreme pallor in contrast to the clerical black clothes he wore, the lank hair under the broad black felt and the slowness and care of his speech. Our rendezvous was the diminutive office of the *Nouvelle Revue Française*, and there he persuaded someone in authority to place back numbers of the review at my disposal. Gide speculated on the possible effect of Whitman's manner upon the form and style of Claudel. One day I received a few pages of examples in which significant phrases had been typed in different-coloured inks.[1]

Gide also gave me a card for M. Valéry Larbaud, whose interest in Whitman was explicit. Upon him I called one afternoon an hour or two after his return from the Mediterranean. In an apartment of exiguous proportions he prepared and served distinctly thin China tea, clotted with cream, which we sipped

---

[1] The question of what *Les Nourritures terrestres* (1897) owed to *Leaves of Grass* was not raised.

as a dissolvant to rolls of granite-like texture, unearthed from a cupboard where they must have matured since my host's departure for the cruise. I seemed to have retained nothing more of this 'interview' except a copy of *Barnabooth*, whose *poésies* in free verse show unmistakable signs of emulation of Whitman's mannerisms and technique, and the visual impression of a short rotund person with a meditative look in his dark glistening eyes.

The *N.R.F.* furnished nothing for my thesis. Indeed, I was beginning to think of Whitman's influence as a will-o'-the-wisp, something that could be mentioned, even glimpsed, but never caught. Yet his name was by now recurring not infrequently in print. M. Duhamel had given me a copy of his *Propos Critiques*, which had appeared in 1912. The first chapter developed a theme which Gide had found in one of Charles-Louis Philippe's letters: 'Maintenant il faut des barbares.' Quoting in French a poem by Whitman which he had chanced upon in a translation of the works of William James, Duhamel comments thus: 'Il n'y a sans doute pas dans le temps actuel, de plus grand introducteur à la vie poétique que Whitman. Il a devancé tous les efforts contemporains dans ce sens. Son exemple est intimidant et généreux.'

In the course of 1913 the *Mercure de France* had been invaded by a discussion of Whitman's morals, stimulated by a fantastic report of the Good Grey Poet's funeral, supposed to have been conveyed by an eye-witness to Guillaume Apollinaire and recorded by him in the number for 1 April. The ceremony was represented as an orgy and invidious constructions were placed on what had been the poet's relations to men and women, though no proof or evidence was supplied. Stuart Merrill defended his compatriot in a letter published in the next number.[1] Other accusations were raised in strident but no more certain tones. To

[1] *Mercure de France*, 16 April 1913.

these Merrill retorted in an article in which, if he did not settle the question, he at least exposed the unreliable basis of the attack.[1]

But the *Mercure* could take Whitman seriously. Reviewing a new edition of the poems of Mallarmé, Duhamel introduces a comparison with Whitman and concludes with a glance at Rimbaud. And so I reach Paris in the winter of 1913 to find the Bard of Manhattan on the one hand abused and derided as an instigator of *mauvaises mœurs*, on the other installed between the most fastidious and the most original of the Symbolist poets.

I. ADRIEN VAN BEVER

To reach number 5, rue de Tournon, I had to cross a cobbled yard of ancient aspect. Thence I was admitted to a small dining-room and through this to a study, a large attractive room, warmed by a stove and containing much furniture, few ornaments, but crowded with yellow-backs. At a table near the door sat a young man with prominent lips, thick black hair and a dull, olive complexion. He turned out to be the son of that eccentric and versatile genius, Charles Cros of *Hareng Saur* fame. Apparently busy correcting proofs, he would chime in at intervals to support the ironies of his senior or to add a note of his own.

At another table near the fire and the window sat Adrien Van Bever, a small man of intriguing appearance with heavy straight brown hair, brushed down over a broad forehead, grave, keen brown eyes and a tiny beard. Rather scrupulously dressed in dark clothes with a white and blue linen shirt-front, cuffs much in evidence, and a large violet-spotted black tie, he had the face of a malicious child of about forty and made me think of Pope quizzing and criticizing everybody between stabs of pain. He

---

[1] 'La Question Walt Whitman', *Mercure de France*, 6 November 1913.

spoke quickly, petulantly, and used slang. Spasmodic gestures punctuated his remarks; he often clutched his knees. 'J'ai des douleurs,' he said the first time. When he moved towards a book or a reference, there was much manoeuvring of his stiffened joints. But nothing impeded the recital of asperities at the expense of contemporaries, a vicious little laugh terminating a thrust at the living or a shrug of the shoulders sealing his disapproval of the dead.

He began by acknowledging my letter. But hadn't it been addressed to the wrong person? He had no information to give about Whitman and could perceive no direct influence from that quarter. Thereupon he digressed on people whose names had already cropped up between us, explaining that someone he happened to be running down at the moment was a friend of his; he was talking only from the literary standpoint, of course, and judging quite dispassionately . . .

The reason for my intrusion was, I explained, a certain passage in one of the notices in the *Poètes d'Aujourd'hui*, of which Van Bever was a co-editor. In this passage, I pointed out, Whitman's name had been pretty definitely connected with the origins of the *vers libre*. My statement seemed to astonish him. He looked up for the reference, read it aloud and then explained without a twinkle that it was his *confrère*, Paul Léautaud, who had written up the notices from notes provided by himself.

Digressions ensued. Kahn, he said, was no poet, though a keen critic. They were not, he admitted, on good terms. 'Nous ne nous entendons pas très bien: en effet nous sommes mal ensemble.' Having nothing in the way of original work to show, Kahn strove to claim as much for himself as possible. He wanted to be made much of and would seize a chance of talking to a foreigner, if he thought it would do his reputation good abroad. He was furious at the treatment he got in *Poètes d'Aujourd'hui*.

In fact the anthology had been something of a curse to its compilers! Everyone mentioned in it thinks he hasn't been given enough space and that too much has been given to others. Most of them, he knew, wished him dead. Kahn had got his talent from pillaging Laforgue. He was legal executor to Laforgue— moral as well—and had made the best use of his friend's genius. Here Cros interposed: Nothing was more unjust than to say that Kahn had invented the *vers libre*.

On rushed the spate of censure, correction and *parti pris*. But what neither of my interlocutors would tell me was, *who* had invented the *vers libre*? Was it Laforgue? Was it Madame Krysinska?

Cros catches at Krysinska. Van Bever won't hear of her. After all, Krysinska's free verse is *prose*, not *verse*, poetry. Baudelaire was the true source with his *petits poèmes en prose*. Yet Baudelaire would probably not have been satisfied with them, had he lived long enough. They were his poetical laboratory. Other pieces of his had been unearthed posthumously, evidently the first drafts of poems. Van Bever was preparing an edition of them; they seemed to be quite unknown. With his love of form Baudelaire would never have been content with these experiments. Yet he had evidently wished to mould a new form midway between poetry and prose. His attempt was conscientious enough; but most of the *poèmes en prose* were not poems at all; they were novelettes, even articles. 'Some, surely, are true poems', interrupts Cros, 'for example *Notre Dame la Lune*.' Agreed: there *were* a few finished poems in the series.

Baudelaire then was the originator. Aloïsius Bertrand was also mentioned, but Bertrand was 'un peu fou'. Baudelaire himself was a bit mad at the end. As for Laforgue, Van Bever didn't seem to have much admiration for him. If Laforgue had lived, he would have despised his work as we know it. Van Bever (this I thought odd) disliked Laforgue's jests at his own expense, his constant mockery of his own sufferings. He must have suffered! The *Chanson du petit hypertrophique* could only have been written by someone who had been through it.

'Bazalgette's the man for you!' But, came the warning, Bazalgette was an enthusiast in a special sense. His case was singular. There was probably no second man like him in France: a meridional with tastes and sympathies strongly Teutonic and Anglo-Saxon. He had begun in the opposite direction as a lover of medieval and Mallarméan types of poetry, that is, with the French tradition. Then, becoming inflamed with the poetry of Germany, he founded the *Revue Internationale* and translated German poems in its columns. His mission had been to enrich French literature by introducing elements from Northern literatures. After his period of Germanic enthusiasm, he turned to England and America and discovered Whitman. His translation of *Leaves of Grass* had been criticized; much of it was *petit nègre*. A new translation of Whitman was needed. No foreign writer could enter into and materially influence French literature until the French themselves can read him in the original. There was little Whitmanian influence: French poets didn't read English.

'The *Unanimistes* are nobodies,' Van Bever continued. 'Romains is the best, Duhamel the worst. Bazalgette would naturally uphold them as illustrating the effect of his translations. But don't imagine a French poet will admit influence of any sort! Be sure, if a French poet tells you he has *not* read a certain book written in his own style, *that's* the book he has at his elbow all day and at his bed-side all night! Yet they *may* admit their debts to you, especially *les jeunes*, for the sake of being mentioned by a foreigner.'

Van Bever was hard on Duhamel. There seemed to be a feud between them over an appointment as critic on the staff of the *Mercure de France*. Duhamel's nomination was a poor joke. Pierre Quillard, who formerly held the post, was a Symbolist with Parnassian leanings. Duhamel had been appointed for a change. He preached and nobody listened.

There was no 'movement' in French literature at the moment. Van Bever could see none; Cros saw none. No contemporary was worth commending.

Vielé-Griffin?—'L'homme le plus désagréable au monde, mais qui a fait des choses intéressantes, quoique toujours avec un peu de raideur.' The reservation referred especially to certain writers who wrote French badly, for example, Verhaeren. Maeterlinck was the first Belgian to write pure French. He had corrected the abundant faults found in his early editions. Both agreed that Vielé-Griffin's French was perfect, save for that touch of *raideur*.

Mallarmé must have known Whitman. Moréas too: he once described him as 'illisible'. Verlaine may have known him—'Here's a fact about Verlaine, something quite unknown, but which appears in his private correspondence. Having read some insignificant Belgian poet who had used certain liberties of phrase, Verlaine noticed how the freedom of rhythm alone had made something interesting out of a mediocre poem.'

Van Bever seemed to have more regard than anyone I met at the time for traditional French literature. Yet he abhorred Boileau—a blot, a dam, a bulwark, a barricade! He didn't seem to have much feeling for the Parnassians or for the poets of the day. His dominant interest at the moment was probably six-teenth-century poetry. He talked much about the noble heritage of French literature. French can never be much influenced by foreign literatures, he thought, having such a tradition of its own.

'You English have a great literature too.' Swift was one of the greatest names in all literature. He had been telling his compatriots for a decade that they ought to know Swift, yet there was no complete translation of his work in French. *Gulliver's Travels* had been translated, of course, but horribly; it was only read by children. 'The French people recognize nothing great, native or foreign—no great idea, style or quality in literature, arts or politics—until it has been not only popularized, brought down to their level, but *ridiculed*, laughed at, turned into a joke and made digestible.'

Van Bever didn't share the admiration for Kipling which I found prevalent and thought his work journalese. Cros mentioned Wells. 'That's not literature at all,' said Van Bever. Then turning to the index of *Poètes d'Aujourd'hui*, he indicated the people he thought I should see. René Ghil would do for one. Giving me his address, he warned me that Ghil was a *fumiste*, but confirmed an impression I had picked up already that he was personally agreeable. Cros thought I should see Paul Fort. The latter had once said in his hearing that he admired Whitman and had been affected by him to some extent. Van Bever scoffed at this notion.

Cros accompanied me downstairs, still bubbling over with views and verdicts. Once outside, he slipped into my hand a card for Paul Fort, repeating what he had said and urging me to use it. I did and was informed by a charming old lady, bowing on her doorstep, that her son was in Russia. Cros, I remember, ran down Henri Guilbeaux's translations from German poets, contrasting them with other renderings in which he seemed to have had a hand. He also spoke of Remy de Gourmont, for whose scholarship he had much admiration. I asked for the critic's address and was given it with a warning not to expect to be invited to call. Thereupon came the customary reference to the disfiguring malady which had made Gourmont decide to live apart, seeing as few people as possible. Cros's prognostication turned out correct. But he had helped me to secure an exquisite autograph.

II. RENÉ GHIL

Through pouring rain I make my way towards the Arc de Triomphe and climb to the fourth storey of a sombre house in the rue Lauriston. Fumbling sounds follow my knock. The door opens on an obscure figure carrying a small red-shaded lamp. We pass through a *salle à manger*, into a comfortable study of an oriental character. Through the gloom emerge the lacquered surface of an octagonal table, a sideboard vaguely like a pagoda and some fine, dark carpets. A large canvas almost covers one of the walls. In the middle of the room stands a big lamp or stove made of red glass threaded with wire, over which is balanced a broad metallic disc or shade with a green bowl poised over the orifice. In it simmers a thick brown paste emitting aromatic odours.

My host's square, swarthy face is set off with a dense mass of jet-black hair, heavy black brows and moustaches. He wears a double-breasted jacket of black cloth, buttoned high at the neck under a vast *lavallière*. Behind on the left stands a bust of himself, by the sculptor Loutschausky, as I afterwards learned.

The impressiveness of Ghil's appearance was softened by a meditative, kindly expression—'sérieuse et d'exquise candeur'—which was difficult to associate with the *fumiste* reputation of this 'Maître de l'École philosophique ou évolutive-instrumentiste'. A phrase I had read somewhere suddenly came to mind:

'Qui est donc celui-ci?' asked Rosny of a friend.

'C'est René Ghil.'

'Ah . . . c'est curieux: il n'en a pas l'air.'

Ghil began with an outline of the development of the *vers libre* —very much 'selon lui'. It would be found summarized in one of his books, *La Poésie Scientifique*, a copy of which he gave me, inscribed with his precise, angular signature. His manner was unostentatious and he could enthuse over other men's work. But he was mainly preoccupied with himself and his theory, attributing much in the origination of free verse and the manner of the Symbolists to his own theses and experiments. All this was done quietly, confidently, without disparagement. He would discuss his contemporaries, flitting from one poet to another with an occasional characterization or dictum, but with no trace of the Parisian fashion of summing up in a word of excessive praise or harsh criticism. 'C'est très curieux!' recurred like a refrain.

Of Mallarmé Ghil spoke as of a divinity. He referred to the Tuesday meetings at the small flat in the rue de Rome—how they used to come away seething with fervour, quivering as if they had seen a vision. He referred with a tremor to the great work Mallarmé had projected. He himself had some notion of the details of its plan. . . .

Vielé-Griffin he considered one of the best poets of the Symbolist school. He was not rightly estimated in France; Ghil didn't know why. The *Mercure de France* had quarrelled with him and had treated him unjustly, because he was a foreigner, perhaps. What an amount of foreign blood there was among the Symbolists! He himself had always attributed Vielé-Griffin's 'sensation brutale', his 'grande ligne lyrique', above all the picturesque element in his work, to Whitman's influence. He referred to one of Griffin's poems about a man walking along a road as very Whitmanian in style.

Verhaeren he adored—'la tendre âme!'—the greatest of living

poets. His enthusiasms, those hallucinations which no one else could experience or represent, those visions, that eye which saw unimaginable things, the eye of a painter too! What an interesting evolution: Parnassian, Symbolist and . . . Instrumentist. Verhaeren's mystical vision was due to his ineradicable religiosity. Talking to Ghil one day he had said with a distress amounting to anguish: 'I agree with all you say, but I can't wrench myself free from this *vieux fonds* of Catholicism which has come down to me from my ancestors.'

Saint-Pol-Roux was really magnificent. He had started with a type of verse which was a *gêne*; he couldn't get into his stride. There were poets who wrote in prose. He was one. His poetic prose was his own and quite original. Moréas too had written some in *Le Thé chez Miranda*.

As for the younger generation, there was no greatness in any of them; no school, no *entente* as of yore, defective as that had been. He had a good word for Vildrac, but regretted the effect Duhamel and Romains were having on him. There was certainly much Whitman in Romains. His *Unanimisme* he had got from two sources, Paul Adam's novel, *Léonine*, and Grégoire le Roy, to whom he owed the word *Unanime*.

Ghil refused to consider Kahn as the originator of the *vers libre*. Kahn's work wasn't strong enough to impose itself. Free verse was a development from Mallarmé (*Un coup de dés*), Verlaine, Vielé-Griffin and himself. Henri de Régnier was a traditionalist. Kahn's free verse was much indebted to Ghil's 'instrumentation verbale' and to Laforgue. The latter was in Germany at the time. Probably under the influence of German and English poetry and also perhaps of Whitman's *Leaves*, he wrote the free verses which he sent to Kahn, who assimilated their principle and ended by claiming authorship of the invention!

No good book had yet been written on Symbolism. He had produced an account of the movement for a Russian review, but it had not been published in French.

Our talk finished with some impressions of Verlaine.[1]

The reminiscences began with the reception of his first book, copies of which had been sent to Mallarmé and Verlaine. The former replied at once, the latter a month later, asking Ghil to go to see him. Somewhere near the Boulevard Voltaire he found a decrepit cabaret and asked the slovenly owner for his lodger. 'Monsieur Paul? Monsieur Paul? Hum, suivez-moi.' The poet was *en déshabillé*. He received his visitor kindly, but expressed distaste for his theory in slang worse than an apache's.

Ghil returned later, when Verlaine was out. Directed to a neighbouring church, he found the poet rapt in silent prayer before a side altar. After a long interval Ghil touched his shoulder. Verlaine's eyes turned in his direction, full of mysterious light and gazing beyond his visitor. Ghil apologised and offered to write. Verlaine resumed his devotions. At length he rose and walked off with his visitor. 'You've got a theory,' he said, 'so have I. Here it is: man is made up of two beings, *un cochon et un ange*. When he's not the one, he's the other. That's my theory.' Suddenly his tone changed: Would it be possible to see Mallarmé? . . . Of course he couldn't think of calling on him. Could Ghil persuade Mallarmé to pay him a visit? Ghil thought he might. But Verlaine had something else in mind. His son was a pupil at the lycée where Mallarmé taught. Did Ghil think Mallarmé would permit his son to come to him? Would Mallarmé *bring* his son? Would Mallarmé, *père de famille, homme convenable*

[1] They had already been published and will be found in *Les Dates et les Œuvres*. I repeat them here in the form in which I took them down because of a few unconventional touches not in the collected version.

avec femme et fille très convenables, come to see him here? Would Ghil ask him to do so?

Ghil received the master's consent and arrangements were made for the meeting. Mallarmé paid a preliminary visit. On the day appointed he came and found Verlaine in clean clothes with a white scarf and his room tidy. They talked. Verlaine's respect was very touching until the conversation got going, when he dropped into slang: 'Eh ben, Mallarmé, on est devenu glorieux!' A day was fixed for bringing his son, but Verlaine relapsed into evil ways and died without having had his wish fulfilled.

III. JEAN ROYÈRE

Middle-sized, considerate, a trifle genteel, with keen, dark eyes; quick of speech though lisping a little; a prominent broad, round head, bald on top. Withal a touch of unconscious dreaminess: his lyrical attitude?

M. Jean Royère begins with information about articles in his review, *La Phalange.* He says (wrongly) that Valéry Larbaud was the first to speak of Whitman in an article which he gives me, emphasizing the author's scholarship and worth. He seems surprised that Larbaud (whom I had seen) had not talked more of his own efforts to popularize Whitman in France; he is too modest.

What was his own attitude to Whitman? — First he will define the object of *La Phalange.* 'C'est une revue par excellence de poésie', founded in July 1906 to unite the younger Symbolist generation to their masters dead or living (to succour the moribund movement, I thought). Among its collaborators are Vielé-Griffin and Verhaeren. Through such men, one an American, the other an unconscious Whitmanian, 'Whitman s'y trouvait naturellement intéressé'.

165

G

Vielé-Griffin had translated, though not for *La Phalange*, one of the finest of the *Leaves*, the threnody for President Lincoln. But he wasn't influenced by his compatriot. Both are poets of life. But Vielé-Griffin 'se rattache à la plus pure poésie française'. He is more 'aesthetic'; doesn't sing the kind of exuberant life that excites Whitman and Verhaeren. Another Whitmanian *d'antan*—one of the first—was Philéas Lebesgue.

He himself has not been touched by such an influence: 'J'aime la poésie par opposition au Whitmanisme.' He claims to be a disciple of Mallarmé and of Verlaine. He withdraws from life, at least from exuberant vitality. For him the poet lives 'dans le calme, contemplant la mort plutôt que la vie'.

Whitman he calls the poet *à la mode*, 'la source la plus riche d'inspiration'. Whitman and Verhaeren have renewed lyrical poetry. 'Ils s'inspirent du spectacle de l'humanité en travail et en souffrance.' Claudel, while resembling Whitman in parts, is very different. In him all this exuberance is corrected by mysticism. 'Le Whitmanisme, c'est un genre trouble, impur, trop de bruit, trop mêlé; un terre à terre sublime.' Claudel has quite a different type of inspiration. He is religious in all senses of the word. 'Il a l'amour de Dieu et l'amour humain.' Claudel has an asceticism which is never found, always refuted, in Whitman. Claudel's form takes more from Rimbaud than from Whitman.

Renderings made from the *Leaves* by Bazalgette had appeared in *La Phalange*. I was advised to ask him for details, also for information about certain poets or *prosateurs* who had written in Whitman's fashion. My interlocutor insisted on a poem about a locomotive, a long, remarkable piece. I couldn't discover whether he meant Whitman's or a French imitation.

M. Royère gave me a copy of his Mallarméan poems, *La Sœur de Narcisse nue*, and a couple of useful numbers of his review.

Before he left we talked a little about form. Each poet should aim at a personal rhythm. The *vers libre* had, he thought, influenced the older rhythm: there had been a sort of reflex action, free verse working back on the rhythm from which it had emerged. But far too much was being made of rhythm at the time. Rhythm isn't something superimposed; it comes unsought with the inspiration. *Language*, not rhythm, was the important thing. Poetry for him was 'l'usage esthétique de la langue, l'emploi de la langue pour créer de la beauté'.

Rimbaud's *Illuminations* he regarded as the 'lieu de naissance' of *vers libre*; they were already free verse.

IV. FRANCIS VIELÉ-GRIFFIN

6-30 p.m. prompt. I reach a row of new elaborate flats on the Quai Passy and climb a flight of huge white steps. The concierge, surprisingly a lady, directs me carefully to the door. It is opened by a valet who leads the way into a large vestibule. He is doubtful whether his master can see me, but I am shown into one of a suite of ornate apartments and then ushered into a study or library which seems immense. It is in terra-cotta, hung with pictures, though not of the modern sort found in the homes of other French poets. One of them over a high chimney-piece is an oval portrait of a general. Round the walls run book-cases filled with splendidly bound volumes. A rich, spacious apartment.

'Visite très différente des autres,' I note, 'un peu décourageante. Ça sent l'Anglo-Saxon.' M. Vielé-Griffin had recently given a *causerie* at the Vieux-Colombier which I had heard. Something parliamentary about his manner, his morning coat, stiff collar and black tie had suggested Mr Haldane.

He comes forward but not with outstretched hand. Had I

come from Oxford?—No, from Aberystwyth.—Where was that?—In Wales.—Here's an ancestor (in oils and gilt) who was also a Welshman. Had I ever met a Gréville?—I had (an impecunious student, but I didn't say so). Relations began to improve.

There was, I should have said, a smartly dressed Frenchman in the room, when I arrived, talking affably of a visit he had paid to England the previous summer, as president of the 'Société des gens de lettres'. He seemed sympathetic and offered to look up a point or two in an obscure review. A few days later I received full details, signed 'Édouard Ducoté'. Now, after a stroll round the room, and having to his host's gratification admired the pictures, he departed.

When we were alone, Vielé-Griffin made a new start in English, but confessing he was out of practice, reverted to French and spoke dogmatically. Whitman's influence in France was nil. The difference in spirit between the French and the Americans was too great. The only poets who were affected by Whitman were Maeterlinck and Claudel. A digression ensued on the situation of art in America, in the course of which I contrived to extract details of translations made from the *Leaves* and published in Symbolist reviews. At last the monologue was running in practical channels.

Vielé-Griffin had been one of the first artisans of the *vers libre* and was one of its most persistent practitioners and propagandists. He now stood with his back to the fire and expounded. The work of the *verslibristes* meant the re-introduction of the tonic accent into French verse. He referred me to the preface to *Christabel* for a similar move in English prosody. Yet Coleridge had given himself unnecessary pains, English having always had accentuation.

Having warmed to his subject, he suddenly seemed to think his argument might be difficult to follow and said he would repeat and explicate at greater length. His intention was to show that the *vers libre* marked the resurrection of something already in the language and literature of France, but suppressed for centuries and forgotten. It was an attempt to bring 'Shelleyism' into French verse. The older forms, the alexandrine, etc., he insisted, were useful only for certain genres: eloquent, narrative, dramatic. The lyrical spirit remained unexpressed. This was largely due to the Renaissance, though it went further back. The *langue d'oc* had a finished art of expression—the lyrical forms of the Troubadours which were organic and native to that tongue. The *langue d'oïl* borrowed these, justifying the accusation that the poetry written in these forms had been artificial from a very early date.

The work of the *verslibristes*, 'our work', was a return to the original inspiration, an effort to get back to its source and re-introduce lyricism into French literature. This amounted to proclaiming the medieval ancestry of modern free verse—not an uncommon theory at the time. Yet when I suggested a more immediate ancestry in the prose-poem and poetic prose, he agreed, but added an amendment. Poetic prose and the prose-poem were not genuine and direct ancestors of the *vers libre* so much as evidences of the feeling for a freer mode now at last fulfilled. Gustave Kahn's *vers libre*, he said, came from the Bible. His own was a natural development, like that of most of the others, from Romantic versification through Verlaine. It marked none the less a revolt from the Parnassian manner and an innovation. In its origins, he affirmed, the *vers libre* had been greatly influenced by English versification. Mallarmé, he added incongruously enough, was influenced by Poe and Verlaine's favourite poet was Tennyson.

As for the younger generation, M. Royère, whom I had seen

a few nights earlier, had expressed his disapproval in clear tones: Duhamel was 'un mauvais poète'. Vielé-Griffin's attitude was a cold antipathy: Duhamel and his group were beneath notice.

The monologue had become spirited and informative. We parted in the grand manner. The master clapped his hands. The valet reappeared. I was shown out.

V. Gustave Kahn

An apartment on the ground floor, full of antiques with a fine old corner-cupboard crammed with curios, a faded suite, a sideboard supporting an elaborate time-piece forming the pedestal of a couple of silver figures; many pictures in impressionistic styles.

M. Kahn was short, thick-set and badly dressed; amiable though not exciting. On my producing a note-book he drew a chair up to the table and spoke in a manner that was decisive, helpful and informative but, though dogmatic, neither self-assertive nor ironical.

Had Whitman any influence?—None at all. Not even on Laforgue?—'I don't know English,' said Kahn, 'Laforgue did. He translated *O Star of France*. But the choice signified nothing. He might have translated any other poet.' Mallarmé knew the American's work. Verlaine didn't. A remark of Mallarmé's was worth remembering. Kahn was present when Louis Le Cardonnel had asked for information about Swinburne and Whitman. Of the latter Mallarmé said by way of definition: 'Il lit le petit journal avec une très belle voix.'

Anxious to bring him out on the *vers libre*, I harped on the two possible modes of origination: a development from Chénier, Hugo and Verlaine, or an innovation starting with the *Palais nomades*. To my surprise, Kahn brushed the latter suggestion aside. There were no innovations in literature. The *vers libre* was a 'logical development'. Such developments or evolutions must be considered deterministically. They had to come somehow. Vigny practised all the innovations introduced by Chénier, though Chénier was unknown to Vigny. And if he had remained unknown, it wouldn't have mattered: Vigny did what Chénier had done before him.

When I tried on the notion of a development from poetic prose, Kahn (like Vielé-Griffin) seemed to respond. He thought it feasible. The transition from prose-poem to *vers libre* was to be seen in some of his own earliest poems published in the *Revue Moderne et Naturaliste* (1879-80), but not collected. These had been written, according to the subject, 'partie en forme versifiée et partie poème en prose'. Lamennais's prose was not 'rythmée'. Real 'prose rythmée' had appeared with Baudelaire. His influence was traceable in three directions—(*a*) 'la perversité': Rolinat, Moréas, etc.; (*b*) Mallarmé, who, at first attempting to 'serrer le vers', ended with *vers libre* (see *Cosmopolis*, 1896-7); (*c*) the Parnassians.

Banville and Leconte de Lisle were responsible for the form adopted by the Parnassian school, which was deplorable. Both were great poets; the fault wasn't theirs. They fashioned a personal form admirably suited to their needs, Banville for his *Odes funambulesques*, Leconte de Lisle 'pour son œuvre statuesque'. It was unfortunate they had so much influence—unfortunate for those who imitated them without having their *fond*.

I risked a query as to Rimbaud's responsibility for the *vers libre*. 'Out of the question,' said Kahn, 'his work wasn't known.'

VI. JULES ROMAINS

The door of the flat was opened by a lady of great beauty, who led the way to a suite of modern rooms *en enfilade*, brilliantly clean and comfortable, done out in chrome and black with the finish of prosperity and taste. M. Romains took me into his study, a darkened room with black carved chairs and settle, a trifle ready-made, perhaps, but elegant and up-to-date.

He was short but striking, with a long nose, black hair and beard, the hair brushed down on his forehead from the centre. He wore a double-breasted navy suit. His movements were quick. He talked with much emphasis; seemed to think what he said was difficult to follow and watched me closely for signs of intelligence. My difficulty was to pretend I always understood. He explained his works, aims and ideas with much fervour and at great length, gazing at me with searching grey eyes.

A chapter of reflections at the end of his book, *Puissances de Paris*, was a sort of résumé of his ideas. But these were best expressed in the *Manuel de Déification*:, 'voilà mes idées directrices'. He mentioned a number of English reviews which had referred to his work, stressing the *Cambridge Magazine* and the interest of Miss Jane Harrison.

He proceeded to point out the general differences between Whitman and himself. Whitman was more individualistic: 'il s'alimente de sa propre flamme'. Romains tended towards the *abnégation* (he used the word in a special sense) of the individual. Instead of the consciousness of the individual, what interested him was 'la conscience du groupe, le centre sensible du groupe'.

These differences were due to nationality. The French hadn't the feeling for individualism found in Anglo-Saxons. The Frenchman was 'peu individualiste' (*sic*). French literature was a proof of this. In it 'c'est l'homme en général qui dit "je" '.

Whitman had other distinctive characteristics, e.g. optimism. 'Nous n'avons pas ce débordant optimisme: nous sommes trop sensibles à l'existence du mal.' Whitman had a veritable cult of democracy. French poets had none of this, or rather democracy to French poets meant something different. 'Chez Whitman il y a un amour naïf du peuple.' This was found only in Vildrac on the French side. With Whitman it was a cult amounting to 'un amour partiel de l'individu'. But to the French, 'le peuple est comme la matière avec laquelle sont faits des ensembles plus intéressants que lui'. This is what 'we' (the *Unanimistes*) were studying: the individuality of the group.

M. Romains read out several passages from the *Manuel de Déification*. Most of them went over my head, but a fragment on the emotions felt in a religious service struck home.

He defended himself stoutly against the charge of writing blank verse. His verse was not blank; it was subtly and entirely new. He read some to illustrate.

This was his method. He takes as basis the alexandrine. Rhyme he abandons, substituting other correspondences; he has attempted some that had never been used in French verse.

His form is a series of verses of the same nature, but not necessarily of twelve syllables. Unequal numbers (*vers impairs*) he often employs, e.g. the nine-syllable line. For rhyme he substitutes 'des rapports, des *accords* de mots', e.g. *mère, mare*. Not assonance, mind! Further, these endings are arranged so as to produce a *transformation*—'une transformation surtout de consonnes'. This method he characterized by the phrase 'utiliser les rapports des prosateurs'; it is an innovation in poetry and is based on sonority—'c'est une sonorité progressive, par exemple *fort, torte*'. Thus in *La Vie Unanime* an effort is made to give each verse 'des terminaisons indéfinies; *mon, moins, mémoire*'.

M. Romains was shocked by the *vers libre*: 'Il lui faut de l'art, une technique qui continue la tradition en la renouvelant.' He was opposed to continual changes of rhythm, because rhythm demanded a succession of similar lines: 'un vers n'est pas un rythme en lui-même'. He insisted again on the need for finding 'de nouveaux rapports' and on looking at rhyme as merely the simplest *rapport*; once again he denied that he wrote blank verse. There were, he said, 'des familles de sons' which must be discovered and used. In his work these new correspondences are employed with considerable freedom. They are found not only at the end of the lines to replace rhyme but often in the middle— end and middle, middle and end—thus making an almost unconscious unity of the poem.

VII. CHARLES VILDRAC

I find M. Charles Vildrac at his *galerie* in the rue de Seine; he invites me in among a forest of impressionist canvases. He is a person of subdued fascinations, slight, fairly tall with long hair, a quiet, intense face, very dark eyes with a wonderful gaze, a black beard and moustaches. He speaks very quietly with hesitation; resents the word 'influence'; prefers *rapprochement* or *concordance*; enumerates some of the ideas which are found now on all hands: the external world, comradeship, etc. Whitman may have been the first to express them. But they couldn't have originated with him; examples of their use are too general.

His own *Livre d'Amour* was written before he had read Bazalgette's translation and none of the poets he knew could read Whitman in the original. He admits a resemblance, an unconscious one, in his feeling for humanity and comradeship, which is something like that found in *Selon ma loi* (*Song of Myself*). He directs me for information to *Propos Critiques* (ch. 1); also to Chennevière's *Printemps* and to Verhaeren. The latter didn't know Whitman before most of his own work was written, not, that is, until the appearance of Bazalgette's translations. Verhaeren and he were once together at a meeting where some of these translations were being read. It was at the Université Populaire, Faubourg St Antoine. On hearing Whitman declaimed for the first time, Verhaeren turned to Vildrac and said, 'C'est du Romains'. I'll find much in Romains's *Vie Unanime*. But this was published before the translations appeared and there is one great difference. *La Vie Unanime* shows much concern with form. Whitman had no such preoccupation; hence his strength, directness and *frusteté*. Whitman took the form nearest to hand and wrote. This would never do in Europe, where tradition demands attention to form.

'Did Whitman influence the special form employed by the *École Unanime*?' I asked. 'Decidedly not!' was the reply. Vildrac owed his own chiefly to Verlaine. He went further, of course; but Verlaine was the great liberator. The origination of the *vers libre*, he admitted, belonged to Laforgue and Kahn; but that was a matter of small importance.

'Could Whitman have influenced the origin of the *vers libre* through Vielé-Griffin and Stuart Merrill?' 'No! See *La Technique nouvelle*. Modern free verse is the natural outcome of Symbolism.'

Henry Franck, my interlocutor added, might very possibly have felt the effect of Whitman's example. He was quite young and started to write at the time when Whitman was beginning to be talked about in France. There was much resemblance, in any case, between the *Leaves* and his *Danse devant l'Arche*. The novels of Charles-Louis Philippe (he wrote no verse) would also provide comparisons. But these were published before Whitman was really known in France. Then, referring to a book of his own in prose, which had just appeared, *Les Découvertes*, M. Vildrac admitted it was quite possible that Whitman had had some effect on that.

VIII. FERNAND GREGH

My appeal had taken some time to elicit a reply. And now I had arrived late for the morning's appointment and stood confronted by unusual difficulties of access. My destination was apparently the twenty-seventh house in the *Hameau* Boulainvilliers, which had to be approached through No. 29, *rue* Boulainvilliers. Finding myself at last before a shabby-looking chalet with a staircase leading to the front door, I had still to wait while movements went on upstairs suggesting ablutions. A bath was evidently being filled; it was well I had not come too early.

I found myself in a large salon full of antiques; in the background a grand piano and a huge tapestry covering an end wall; near the fire a gilt lectern surmounted by an eagle; furniture in several styles, mostly bluish-white and much worn; curtains and ornaments rather tawdry; pictures in oils—all suggesting a loose, picturesquely untidy host. In walks a handsome, pleasant-looking man, most elegantly dressed, who greets me almost with warmth. He sits at a bureau. From a couch nearby I survey a noble head, bald but with very fine black curls floating behind, an aquiline nose, a lovely olive complexion, intensely black eyes, a monocle and a square curly black beard. Also the light brown suit with low-cut waistcoat, showing off a dark green, patterned tie, dazzling linen and fashionable *bottines* with fawn tops. Perfect ease and grace of manner.

Whitman, M. Gregh thought, must have had a considerable influence on the formation of the *vers libre* through Vielé-Griffin and Stuart Merrill—that excellent, underestimated poet—and also through translations. The literary élite had known Whitman for twenty years; he laughed at the idea of their having had to wait for Bazalgette's translation. Moreover there had always been a *vers libre.* See La Fontaine, a certain *cantate* of Jean-Baptiste Rousseau, the poetry of the Middle Ages, even Lamartine's canticles in *Les Harmonies* . . .

Modern *vers libre* was first written by Marie Krysinska and Gustave Kahn. Kahn's work was of no importance and had gone unnoticed. 'Did Kahn write free verse before Laforgue?' I asked. Gregh didn't know—no one knew! After Kahn came Vielé-Griffin, Moréas and Verhaeren, Rimbaud's being poetic prose.

Whitman, M. Gregh continued, was now exerting a strong influence on Romains and his group. The group itself was negligible—quite young men—though Romains was *très doué.*

As to formative influences, Kahn was a Jew. His dominant source of inspiration had been the Bible—as it was for Claudel. The *vers libre* also owed something to Anglo-Saxon influence through Mallarmé and Verlaine. Its source had certainly been 'la prose lyrique'. The great object of the *verslibristes* had been, at the earliest period, to abstract from this lyrical prose the essence of poetry and to suppress the prose: 'Peu à peu chez Régnier, chez Verhaeren, chez Stuart Merrill, cette prose lyrique a éliminé les éléments non-rythmiques, et elle est devenue le vrai vers libre, c'est à dire nous écrivons de vrais vers quelquefois de quatorze pieds.'

Twice or thrice M. Gregh illustrated points by reading from a volume on his bureau. It was one of his own books of verse and he promised to send me a copy. It came.

Talk turned on music and poetry. How close was the connection between music and free verse! All his own work had been influenced by music. His father had been a musician.

Could the *vers libre* have come from Verlaine and Mallarmé? He shrugged his shoulders at my persistence. How difficult the matter was! He thought not, for neither had written free verse and Verlaine had declared against it.

Some reference to the indebtedness of these poets to England turned the talk on our country in relation to France. A close bond of friendship should always exist between the two. They couldn't be considered as sister nations because of the difference of blood, but they were 'deux peuples frères d'humanité'. France had always drawn deeply from English literature, which she found more original and more assimilable than that of Germany.

Something was said about liberalism in literature and politics, and M. Gregh asked about Lloyd George. Was the present-day tendency liberal or conservative? He himself didn't know English but his wife read it easily and acted as interpreter. What was the present state of English poetry? I mentioned Masefield, Watson, Bridges, Francis Thompson. What was the poetic status of Kipling? My reply seemed to surprise him. M. Gregh observed that Kipling's *Ode to France* had been translated and French poets and authors, including Anatole France and himself, had found it good. The ideas, the thoughts expressed in it were very fine. He himself had responded with a poem published in one of the reviews. But they had all been startled and amused to learn that in England the *Ode to France* was considered by no means a great poem, nor its author a great poet!

IX. Henri Guilbeaux

Bazalgette had told me of Henri Guilbeaux, lending me an essay of his which I found useful, but intimating that the author was not yet a great poet.

The room I lived in was in darkness when he arrived. On lighting up I perceived a young man of perhaps twenty-six, pale and rather slight, with blue eyes, light yellow locks in abundance and a blond curly beard. Affable, voluble, enthusiastic, with keen, flashing glances and eloquent gestures.

We are at once on easy terms. I start by explaining my work, but am soon absorbed in hearing an account of his. What a life he had led! Very hard work with all the world against him. The monologue runs on tumultuously, covering much of the surface of Europe in the course of an hour. It turns on two principal topics: Henri Guilbeaux himself and the 'secret service' of less reputable French poets.

Guilbeaux's parents had objected to his following a literary career. He had had to work with his hands as a factory engineer. The poetry of machines had always impressed him; he was never happier than in a machine room. That was in Belgium, his 'pays d'origine'. One day someone gave him a copy of *Les Villes tentaculaires*. It was a self-revelation. These things, then, had a beauty of their own. What he had dreamt of doing had been done by someone else. He avowed an excessive, an *imitative* worship of Verhaeren.

He had been much in Germany; knew the language and loved the people; had done what he could to bring about a *rapprochement*; had studied the modern German poets and made an anthology of French translations to which Verhaeren had written a preface. He had been struck by the influence Whitman and Verhaeren were exerting in Germany as well as in France, where they were the twin sources of inspiration. He had spent much time at Berlin and written his first book there, *Les Gares de Berlin*, which he admitted to be pure Verhaeren.

He had read a little Whitman in English. But it was Bazalgette's translation that had revealed Whitman to him and had made him an ardent Whitmanite. From his portfolio he takes a few journals containing reviews of articles and lectures he had written on the

topic. At present he finds Whitman more inspiring than Verhaeren and less literary; he accuses the latter of writing 'literature'
in *Les Blés mouvants*. The Belgian poet must have known Whitman
—at least he had once heard him say that Bazalgette's translation
was as good as the original. But most of the inspiration of *Les
Villes tentaculaires* came from London.

He himself was interested in the life of the people—a socialist
with anarchist tendencies. For this he was not very acceptable
to many of his contemporaries. Anarchist friends had persuaded
him to write in favour of a man who had been unjustly condemned; the result of the campaign was that he himself had
become suspect. Another cause of his countrymen's antipathy
was that he loved Germany and was doing what he could to bring
about amicable relations between that country and France.

Many tales followed of the animosities existing between the
younger generations of French poets. Guilbeaux's opposition
to his contemporaries in the literary field was grounded in the
belief that they had all too much brain. He seemed to be suffering
from a kind of anti-literary phobia. *La Vie Unanime* was, he
thought, with Franck's *Danse devant l'Arche*, the greatest book
that had appeared for the last ten years, but he jibbed at Romains's
'cerebralism'. Ideas and lyricism never went together. Romains
was too much of a thinker, of a philosopher. He and Duhamel
were 'des intellects de cabinet', their work smelt of the lamp;
not enough of their inspiration came from 'la vie active'. Claudel
was influenced in his ideas, images and form by Whitman. Yet
he must be classed with Romains, who resembled Claudel more
closely than he did Whitman. Claudel was characterized as 'une
personnalité minime, ayant plus de cérébralité que de personnalité, que d'individualité'.

For another contemporary, Nicolas Baudouin, Guilbeaux

had no respect. As Baudouin and his group have long ceased to be heard of, I needn't relate how badly he appeared to have treated Guilbeaux. The latter left me with a bundle of manuscripts to look at, unmitigated Whitman-Verhaerenese. But it had been an exhilarating couple of hours, and when after the war I read of the difficulties Henri Guilbeaux had got himself into with the French Government, I recalled this interview and its sequel— an account of my youthful investigations occupying half a column of *Le Temps* and signed by my fervent interlocutor of long ago.

X. ÉMILE VERHAEREN

My visit to Verhaeren at St Cloud in February 1914 was an amusing and instructive affair, which I have already attempted to describe (*Message*, June 1944). From humorously recounting his sojourns in England the poet could not be diverted by tentative inquiries about 'ce bonhomme Whitman'. This quest of influences had gone too far. He defended one of his own poems from the implication that Nietzsche had inspired it by relating how Georg Brandes had directed his attention to the works of the philosopher after the poem had been published. Proofs were laid before me; I felt admonished. And perhaps it would be well to pause and consider the scene that might ensue in some academic hereafter, if all those poets, painters and musicians convicted of borrowing from their kind could confront their accusers and the final accounts of the *comparatiste* movement were histrionically wound up.

BIBLIOGRAPHIES

The following lists are of works mentioned in the text, with a few titles of more recent works of specific interest.

I FRENCH BOOKS

[Place of publication is not given when it is Paris. M.F.=Mercure de France; N.R.F.=Nouvelle Revue française (Gallimard).]

Baldensperger, F. *Orientations Etrangères chez H. de Balzac.* Champion. 1922.

Balzac, H. de *Œuvres Complètes.* Michel Lévy. 1870. Esp. vol. XVII.

Banville, T. de *Petit Traité de Poésie française.* Charpentier. 1894.

Barre, A. *Le Symbolisme.* Jouve. 1912.

Baudelaire, C. *Œuvres Complètes*, édition critique par F. F. Gautier, continuée par Y. G. Le Dantec. N.R.F. 1918-1937.

   Œuvres Complètes, édition critique par J. Crépet. Conard. 1922-1939.

   Les Œuvres de Charles Baudelaire (Pléiade édition). Texte établi et annoté par Y. G. Le Dantec. 2 vols. N.R.F. 1931-32.

   Les Fleurs du Mal, édition critique par J. Crépet et G. Blin. Librairie José Corti. 1942.

   Les Fleurs du Mal, edited by E. Starkie. Blackwell. Oxford. 1943.

   Les Petits Poèmes en Prose, edited with a preface by E. Raynaud. Garnier. 1928.

Lettres (1841-1866). M.F. 1907.

Correspondance Générale. Conard. 1947.

Bazalgette, L. *Walt Whitman, l'Homme et son Œuvre.* M.F. 1908.

   Les Feuilles d'herbe. (trans. of *Leaves of Grass*). M.F. 1909.

Béguin, A. *L'Ame romantique et le Rêve.* Marseille. 1937.

Béranger, H. *L'Ame moderne.* 1892.

Bertrand, L. (Aloïsius). *Gaspard de la Nuit.* Labitte. 1842.

Bidal, M. L. *Les Ecrivains de l'Abbaye.* Boivin. s.d.

Blémont, É. *Beautés étrangères.* Lemerre. 1904.

Blin, G. *Baudelaire*, avec une préface de J. Crépet. N.R.F. 1939.

Chateaubriand, R. de *Le Génie du Christianisme.* 2 vols. Firmin-Didot. 1874.

Champion, P. *Marcel Schwob et son temps.* Grasset. 1927.

Claudel, P. *Tête d'Or.* Libr. Art Indép. 1890.

   Cinq Grandes Odes. N.R.F. 1913.

   Positions et Propostions. N.R.F. (1928). 1934. 2 vols. (Esp. vol. 1. 'Réflexions et propositions sur le vers français'.)

Clapton, G. T. *Baudelaire et De Quincey*, Les Belles Lettres. 1931.

Constant (Abbé). *Les Trois Harmonies.* 1845.

Del Gir, R. *Le Vers Libre, ou les règles de l'assonance.* Le Ménure, 1950.

Della Rocca de Vergalo (*See* Vergalo).

Duhamel, G. *Notes sur la Technique poétique* (with C. Vildrac). Figuière. 1910. New edition. Champion. 1926.

   Propos Critiques. Figuière. 1912.

   Le Temps de la Recherche. Hartmann. 1948.

Dujardin, É. *Les Premiers Poètes du Vers Libre.* M.F. 1922. *Mallarmé par un des Siens.* Messein. 1936.

Ferran, A. *L'Esthétique de Baudelaire*. Hachette. 1933.

Franck, H. *La Danse devant l'Arche*. N.R.F. 1912.

Gautier, J. *Le Livre de Jade*. Lemerre. 1867.

Ghil, R. *Les Dates et les Œuvres*. Crès . 1912.

    Tradition de la Poésie scientifique. Soc. Lit. Fr. 1920.

Gide, A.   *Prétextes*. M.F. 1903. (Esp. *De l'Influence en Littérature.*)

Gourmont, R. de *Le Livre des Masques*. M.F. 1896.

    Le IIe Livre des Masques. M.F. 1898.

    L'Esthétique de la Langue française. M.F. 1899.

    Le Problème du Style. M.F. 1902.

    Promenades Littéraires. 5 vols. M.F. 1904-1928.

Grammont, M. *Le Vers français*. Picard. 1904. New editions, Champion, 1912 and 1926.

Henriot, E. *A quoi rêvent les jeunes gens*. Champion. 1912.

Henry, M. L. *Stuart Merrill*. Champion. 1927.

Huret, J. *Enquête sur l'Evolution littéraire*. Charpentier. 1891.

Hytier, J. *Les Techniques Modernes du Vers français*. Presses Universitaires. 1923.

Hugo, V. *Les Misérables*. (1862). Ollendorf. 1912.

Huysmans, J. K. *A Rebours*. Charpentier. 1884.

Kahn, G. *Premiers Poèmes, avec une préface sur les vers libres*. M.F. 1897.

    Symbolistes et Décadents. Messein. 1902.

Laforgue, J. *Œuvres Complètes: Poésies*. M.F. 1903.

Lamartine, A. de *Méditations Poétiques*, 2 vols. Hachette. 1915.

Lamennais, F. *Paroles d'un Croyant*. Renduel. 1833.

Larbaud, V. *Barnabooth*. N.R.F. 1913.

Le Blond, M. *Essai sur le Naturisme.* M.F. 1896.

Le Cardonnel (G)
et Vellay (C). *La Littérature contemporaine.* M.F. 1905.

Lemonnier, L. *Edgar Poe et la critique française.* 1928.

  Les Traducteurs d'Edgar Poe en France. Presses Universitaires. 1928.

  Edgar Poe et les poètes français. Nouvelle Revue Critique. 1932.

Lévi, Éliphas. (See Constant.)

Maeterlinck, M. *Serres Chaudes.* Vanier. 1889.

Maistre, J. de *Les Soirées de St-Pétersbourg.* 2 vols. Nicolle. 1821.

Mallarmé, S. *Un coup de dés.* N.R.F. 1914.

  Divagations, Fasquelle. 1897. New edition with preface by E. M. Souffrin, Fasquelle. 1943.

Martino, P. *Parnasse et Symbolisme.* Colin. 1925.

Mauclair, C. *L'Art en Silence.* Ollendorf. 1901.

Mendès, C. *Le Mouvement poétique français jusqu'en 1900.* Fasquelle. 1903.

Merrill, S. *Les Quatre Saisons.* M.F. 1900.

Mockel, A. *Propos de littérature.* Libr. Art Indép. 1894.

Mondor, H. *Vie de Mallarmé.* N.R.F. 1941.

Nerval, G. de *Les Illuminés.* Lecou. 1852.

  Aurélia, ou le rêve et la vie. Payot. 1913.

Morice, C. *La Littérature de tout à l'heure.* Perrin. 1889.

Morier, H. *Le Rythme du vers libre symboliste.* 3 vols. (1. Verhaeren; 2. H. de Régnier; 3. Vielé-Griffin). Éditions critiques. Geneva. 1943-44.

Noulet, E. *L'Œuvre poétique de Stéphane Mallarmé.* Droz. 1940.

Patterson, A. S. *L'Influence d'Edgar Poe sur Charles Baudelaire.* Grenoble. 1903.

Pommier, J. *La Mystique de Baudelaire.* Les Belles Lettres. 1932.

Raymond, M. *De Baudelaire au Surréalisme.* Corréa. 1933.

Raynaud, E. *La Mêlée Symboliste.* 3 vols. Renaissance du Livre. 1918-1922. See Baudelaire (*Les Petits Poèmes en Prose*).

Retté, A. *Le Symbolisme, anecdotes et souvenirs.* Messein. 1903.

Rimbaud, A. *Œuvres, vers et prose.* M.F. 1912.

    Lettres de la vie littéraire. N.R.F. 1931.

Romains, J. *La Vie Unanime.* L'Abbaye. 1908. M.F. 1913.

    Petit traité de versification (avec G. Chennevière). N.R.F. 1924.

Saint-Martin, C. de *Le Ministère de l'Homme esprit.* 1802.

Sarrazin, G. *La Renaissance de la Poésie anglaise.* 1899.

Seylaz, L. *Edgar Poe et les premiers Symbolistes français.* Lausanne. 1923.

Souza, R. de *Du Rythme en français.* Welter. 1912.

Spire, A. *Plaisir Poétique et Plaisir Musculaire, essai sur l'évolution des techniques poétiques.* Vanni, New York and Corti, Paris. 1949.

Tancrède de Visan. *L'Attitude du Lyrisme Contemporain.* M.F. 1911.

Thieme, H. P. *Essai sur l'Histoire du Vers français.* Champion. 1916.

Touche, D. de la *Abrégé des ouvrages d'Emmanuel Swedenborg' contenant la doctrine de la nouvelle Jérusalem céleste, précédé d'un Discours où l'on examine la vie de l'auteur, le genre de ses écrits et leur rapport au temps présent.* Treuttel. Strasbourg. 1788. (Published simultaneously at Stockholm.)

Valéry, P. *Variété* II. N.R.F. 1924.

Van Bever (A)
et Léautaud (P). *Poètes d'Aujourd'hui*, 3 vols. M.F. 1942.

Vergalo, Della R. de *La Poétique nouvelle.* 1880.

Verhaeren, E. *Les Villes tentaculaires, précédées des Campagnes hallucinées.* M.F. 1904.

Les Blés mouvants. M.F. 1912.

Verlaine, P. *Œuvres Complètes.* Vanier. 1899-1903.

Viatte, A. *Les Sources Occultes du Romantisime.* Champion. 1928.

Victor Hugo et les Illuminés de son temps. Montreal. 1942.

Vielé-Griffin, F. *Joies.* Tresse et Stock. 1889.
Poèmes et Poésies. M.F. 1895.

Clarté de Vie. M.F. 1897.

Vildrac, C. *Le Vers librisme, étude critique sur la forme poétique irrégulière.* Ed. de la Revue Mauve. 1902.

Notes sur la Technique poétique (see Duhamel).

Les Découvertes. N.R.F. 1912.

Livre d'Amour. N.R.F. 1914.

Villiers de l'Isle-Adam, A. *Axël*, Quantin, 1890.

II English Books

(Place of publication is not given when it is London.)

Bithell, J. *Maurice Maeterlinck.* Walter Scott. 1913.

Cambriaire, C. P. *The Influence of E. A. Poe.* Stechert. New York. 1927.

Castiglioni, A. *Adventures of the Mind.* Sampson Low. 1947.

Clayton, V. *The Prose-Poem in French Literature of the Eighteenth Century.* Columbia University. New York. 1936.

De la Mare, W. *Early one Morning.* Faber. 1935.

De Quincey, T. *Confessions of an Opium Eater.* (Temple Classics.) 1899.

Emerson, R. W. *Works.* Esp. vol. IV. ('Representative Men'.) Macmillan. 1883.

Encyclopædia Britannica (9th edition).

Faber, G. *The Oxford Apostles.* Faber. 1933; revised edition, 1936; cheap edition, 1951.

Fausset, H. l'A. *Walt Whitman, Poet of Democracy.* Cape. 1942.

Feuillerat, A. *Baudelaire et la Belle aux cheveux d'or.* Yale Univ. Press. New York. 1941.

Hunt, H. J. *The Epic in Nineteenth-Century France.* Blackwell. Oxford. 1941. (Chap. II. gives a good short account of Illuminism and its influence in France.)

Huxley, A. *Vulgarity in Literature,* Chatto and Windus. 1930.

Jones, P. M. *Emile Verhaeren,* Univ. of Wales Press Board and H. Milford. 1926. (Esp. chap. VI. 'The Transition in Technique'.)

Lawrence, D. H. *Studies in Classical American Literature.* Martin Secker. 1924.

Lehmann, A. G. *The Symbolist Aesthetic in France.* Blackwell. Oxford. 1950. (Esp. references to the *Vers libre.*)

Lowes, J. L. *The Road to Xanadu.* Constable. 1927.

Murry, J. M. *Discoveries.* Cape. 1924.

Oxford Book of French Verse. Clarendon Press. Oxford. 1936.

Poe, E. A. *Complete Poetical Works, with three Essays on Poetry.* Henry Frowde. 1909.

Selincourt, B. de *Blake.* Duckworth. 1909.

Shanks, E. *Edgar Allan Poe.* Macmillan. 1937.

Starkie, E. *Baudelaire.* Gollancz. 1933.

Les Fleurs du Mal, edited by E. Starkie. Blackwell. Oxford. 1943.

Arthur Rimbaud. Heinemann. 1947.

Swedenborg, E. *The Future Life (Heaven and Hell).* J. Speirs. 1882.

The True Christian Religion. Swedenborgian Society, 1873.

Swinburne, A. C. *Prose Works.* Vol. v. Heinemann. 1926.

Symons, A. *The Symbolist Movement in Literature.* Heinemann. 1899.

Thompson, V. *French Portraits.* Badger. Boston. 1900.

Tillyard, E. M. W. *The Elizabethan World Picture.* Chatto and Windus. 1943.

Whitman, Walt. *Leaves of Grass* (Camden Booklovers' edition). Putman. New York. 1900.

Complete Prose Works. Putnam. New York. 1902.

Œuvres choisies (translations by several hands). N.R.F. 1918.

Wordsworth, W. *The Prelude,* edited by E. de Selincourt. Humphrey Milford. 1926.

Yeats, W. B. *Autobiographies: The Trembling of the Veil.* Macmillan. 1926.

INDEX TO PROPER NAMES

INDEX TO PERIODICALS

(Full references will be found on the pages indicated below.)

196